NEW DIRECTIONS FOR TEACHING AND LEARNING

Robert J. Menges, *Northwestern University*
EDITOR-IN-CHIEF

Marilla D. Svinicki, *University of Texas, Austin*
ASSOCIATE EDITOR

# Mentoring Revisited: Making an Impact on Individuals and Institutions

Marie A. Wunsch
*University of Wisconsin*

EDITOR

Number 57, Spring 1994

JOSSEY-BASS PUBLISHERS
San Francisco

MENTORING REVISITED: MAKING AN IMPACT ON INDIVIDUALS
AND INSTITUTIONS
Marie A. Wunsch (ed.)
New Directions for Teaching and Learning, no. 57
Robert J. Menges, Editor-in-Chief
Marilla D. Svinicki, Associate Editor

Microfilm copies of issues and articles are available in 16mm and 35mm,
as well as microfiche in 105mm, through University Microfilms Inc., 300
North Zeeb Road, Ann Arbor, Michigan 48106-1346.

LC 85-644763          ISSN 0271-0633          ISBN 0-7879-9973-3

NEW DIRECTIONS FOR TEACHING AND LEARNING is part of The Jossey-Bass
Higher and Adult Education Series and is published quarterly by Jossey-
Bass Inc., Publishers, 350 Sansome Street, San Francisco, California
94104-1342. Second-class postage paid at San Francisco, California, and
at additional mailing offices. POSTMASTER: Send address changes to New
Directions for Teaching and Learning, Jossey-Bass Inc., Publishers, 350
Sansome Street, San Francisco, California 94104-1342.

SUBSCRIPTIONS for 1994 cost $47.00 for individuals and $62.00 for institutions, agencies, and libraries.

EDITORIAL CORRESPONDENCE should be sent to the editor-in-chief, Robert J.
Menges, Northwestern University, Center for the Teaching Professions,
2003 Sheridan Road, Evanston, Illinois 60208-2610.

Cover photograph by Richard Blair/Color & Light © 1990.

# CONTENTS

FROM THE SERIES EDITORS

*About This Publication.* Since 1980, *New Directions for Teaching and Learning (NDTL)* has brought a unique blend of theory, research, and practice to leaders in postsecondary education. We continue to work to uphold *NDTL*'s reputation not only for solid substance but also for timeliness, compactness, and accessibility.

These are our goals for the series: (1) To inform our readers about current and future directions in teaching and learning. (2) To illuminate the context that shapes those new directions. (3) To illustrate new directions through examples taken from real settings. (4) To propose how new directions can be incorporated into still other settings.

This publication reflects our view that research and writing on teaching deserved respect as a high form of scholarship. We believe that significant scholarship is done not only by the researcher who reports results of studies but also by the practitioner who shares with others disciplined reflections on teaching. Contributors to *NDTL* approach questions of teaching and learning as seriously as they approach substantive questions in their own disciplines, dealing not only with pedagogical issues but also with the intellectual and social context out of which those issues arise. Authors deal with both theory to practice and back again.

*About This Volume.* In this volume of *NDTL*, Marie A. Wunsch discusses the theory and context of the practice of mentoring and the variables that influence its success. The real-life practice is then illustrated in a wide range of settings with a wide range of participants, from students to faculty. She ends this volume with a set of philosophical and pragmatic questions that a person contemplating a mentoring program should address.

Robert J. Menges, *Editor-in-Chief*
Marilla D. Svinicki, *Associate Editor*

*Robert J. Menges, editor-in-chief, is professor of education and social policy at Northwestern University, and senior researcher, National Center on Post-secondary Teaching, Learning, and Assessment.*

*Marilla D. Svinicki, associate editor, is director of the Center for Teaching Effectiveness, University of Texas at Austin.*

# EDITOR'S NOTES

In the past decade few strategies for personal and professional advancement have received as much public attention as mentoring. Since Levinson, Darrow, Klein, Levinson, and McKee (1978), Kanter (1977), and Sheehy (1979) popularized the notion that adults go through continuous passages or periods of growth and change, attention has been drawn to the significant role of patrons, advocates, role models, coaches, guides, collaborators, and mentors in the process of personal and professional development. The concept of mentoring as a means of easing the passage into young adulthood (albeit in this case only of a young male) is as old as Homer's *Odyssey* (ninth century B.C.) in the Western world. The Confucian tradition (sixth century B.C.) draws on mentoring as a means of developing academic and bureaucratic leaders. However, the planned use of structured mentoring as a strategy for personal advancement and success in complex organizations is a recent phenomenon and a particularly American one.

The American corporate sector quickly took up Levinson and others as the gurus of career development (at least for men) and incorporated (and even flaunted) mentoring as the tool of choice to reach the executive suite. As women and minorities sought equal opportunity for advancement, mentoring received added attention as an equalizer in breaking barriers to the development of underutilized groups. From 1980 to 1990, over 380 articles appeared in the popular press and academic journals on mentoring in business and education. In retrospect, the majority appear to be engaging in "mentoring hype." Mentoring has emerged as a "quick fix" to success. Supposedly, it is easily set up and naturally done with skill and enthusiasm. In fact, little of this perception is accurate and much of what passes for "mentoring" is not mentoring at all.

What happened when mentoring was taken up by higher education? Some academicians would say mentoring *always* existed in higher education, particularly in the relationship between a faculty member and a student. Faculty easily relate to the roles of guide, patron, and counselor to students. Many do engage in productive informal mentoring with protégés of their choice. Among faculty ranks, many academics would tell us that mentoring goes on "naturally." Senior colleagues normally pass on the written and unwritten wisdom and lore of academe to their juniors. Graduate students and new faculty are thus socialized into the profession and the community of scholars, and success and advancement follows. But does it? How do we know? Who gets mentored? Who benefits? What specific techniques are most effective? How do mentors learn their mentoring skills? Do mentees require help in using mentoring effectively? Does the institution benefit from individuals being mentored?

A growing body of literature and research confirms that there are as many theories about mentoring as there are personal experiences of it. There is no universally accepted definition of mentoring and there is a good deal of "magical thinking" about what happens when mentors and mentees do come together. Until recently there has been little attempt to assess mentoring processes or their impact on individuals and institutions. Research and evaluation still rely heavily on retrospective, self-reporting by persons who experienced positive mentoring. Data-based research as yet does not definitively confirm the value of or the need for mentoring (Carmin, 1988). There is also a growing subtext of anecdotal information from individuals who experienced informal mentoring, but who indicate that it does not always happen in a systematic and productive way. For many women and minority students and faculty mentoring does not happen at all.

Yet none of this means that mentoring should not be done. What it does mean is that more attention needs to be given to planned mentoring that places the process in the wider context of institutional mission and goals and of the academic culture, and that assesses the relationship between individual and institutional vitality.

"Planned," "structured," or "formal" mentoring programs proliferated in higher education during the 1980s in conjunction with concerns over the progress and attrition of minority students. Colleges and universities intensified efforts to retain high-risk students who fail because of rejection, cultural isolation, confusion about academic goals, frustration with the bureaucratic environment, and an academic culture deeply imbedded with Western white male values (Terrell and Wright, 1988; Pascarella, 1980). In an attempt to replicate what appeared to be successful mentoring of professionals in the workplace, colleges and universities attempted compensatory or enrichment mentoring programs to break the barriers to recruitment, retention, tenure, and promotion for minority and women faculty.

Formal mentoring programs have now become a regular component of new student and faculty development and support activities on many campuses. Mentoring may also focus on special target groups, such as nontraditional students, women students in science, predoctoral minority students, teaching assistants, or junior faculty. Some mentoring (although it may not be called so) is being done to ease middle-aged and senior faculty through career changes and into retirement.

This volume on mentoring in higher education attempts to accomplish several goals. In Part One, mentoring is placed in an *academic* context and emphasis is put on creating an academic community that understands the complexity of mentoring students and faculty through academic passages, be this completing a degree, developing as competent teachers and scholars, or attaining promotion, tenure, or retirement. In Chapter One, Marie A. Wunsch proposes enlarging the dialogue on mentoring by placing it in the context of the academic culture where there can be a convergence of individual and institutional values and goals for human development. Chapter Two continues the broad view of mentoring as a complex adult development process as Mary L. Otto makes the case that the mentoring relationship evolves over time and that the mentor, protégé, and institution can change and grow as a result.

While staff and administrators certainly are part of the academic institution, their development is not addressed here. The definition of staff varies so greatly by academic institution that it is difficult to determine mentoring as a consistent component of staff development activities. The recent work of Green (*Investing in Higher Education: A Leadership Handbook* [ACE, 1991]) includes a comprehensive analysis of mentoring and development programs for college and university administrators.

Part Two illustrates that effective mentoring in academe requires and institutional context and support system that is considerably different than those in the corporate model. A variety of mentoring program models are presented that may be replicable in colleges and universities seeking guidance in implementing mentoring programs. These programs are set in different types of institutions (research, doctoral, and comprehensive universities and liberal arts colleges) and focus on different groups (undergraduate, graduate, and minority students, and junior, female, minority, adjunct, and senior faculty). In Chapter Three, Marie A. Wunsch presents an overview of the major themes and issues to be considered in developing or enhancing a mentoring program. All the program models illustrate these components in their organization and practices.

In Chapter Four, Melvin C. Terrell and R. Kipp Hassell present an overview of mentoring programs for undergraduate minority students, and the results of a national survey of existing programs and their characteristics. They then go on to describe a model university program that represents this type of mentoring. In Chapter Four, Keith B. Wilson details the challenges of beginning a mentoring program for at-risk freshmen in a small open-admissions liberal arts college. Giving attention to the careers of junior faculty women through mentoring is the subject of Chapter Six, written by Linda K. Johnsrud. William K. Jackson and Ronald D. Simpson take on the task, in Chapter Seven, of describing two mentoring programs that help new faculty develop as both teachers and scholars. In Chapter Eight, Barbara J. Millis shows that peer mentoring is an effective process for colleagues to help part-time faculty develop as teachers and fuller members of the academic community. In Chapter Nine, Kay U. Herr places discipline-focused mentoring for faculty within the context of the responsibility of the academic department. In Chapter Ten, Daniel W. Wheeler and B. J. Wheeler focus on mentoring midcareer and senior faculty through changes in life and career.

Part Three offers a series of personal narratives to allow the mentoring experience to take on a human face. In Chapters Eleven through Thirteen, five individuals discuss how they experienced mentoring or designed a mentoring experience that respected their own ethnic and cultural backgrounds.

In Chapter Eleven, James Bonilla, Carlton Pickron, and Travis Tatum trace their own educational backgrounds as men of color and how they addressed their need for mentoring when it was not available to them in the educational system from elementary through graduate school. In Chapters Twelve and Thirteen, Virgie O. Chattergy and Christine A. Stanley describe very personal journeys through mentoring as graduate students that accommodated their unique ethnic, cultural, and gender characteristics.

Finally, the Appendix provides a checklist that will serve as a guide for those who wish to develop a structured mentoring program.

Berquist (1992) sees the "developmental culture" of the academic institution as bridging the gap between the needs of the individual and the requirements of the institution itself. If we believe that the welfare of individuals and the organization are one and the same, the points of compatibility and mutual support must be found and nurtured. The concerns of individuals for growth, change, advancement, recognition, and support can be brought into harmony with the organizational goals for continuity, stability, and community.

Astin (1974) and Berquist and Phillips (1975) associated this convergence of goals with the growth of the faculty development movement in the 1970s. The twenty-first century will bring similar and new challenges to higher education. Bureuacratic institutions must renew their responsibility to support the developmental needs of staff, students, and faculty and recognize the relationship between personal change and organizational vitality. An integrated, comprehensive model of human and organizational development which includes mentoring for faculty, staff, students, and administrators will be significant in community building and institutional revitalization.

Marie A. Wunsch
Editor

### References

Astin, A. *Faculty Development in Times of Retrenchment.* San Francisco: Jossey-Bass, 1974.

Berquist, W. H. *The Four Cultures of the Academy: Insights and Strategies for Improving Leadership in Collegiate Organizations.* San Francisco: Jossey-Bass, 1992.

Berquist, W. H., and Phillips, S. A. *A Handbook for Faculty Development,* vol. 1. Washington, D. C.: Council of Independent Colleges, 1975.

Carmin, C. N. "Issues in Research on Mentoring: Definitional and Methodological." *International Journal of Mentoring,* 1988, 2, 9–13.

Kanter, R. M. *Men and Women in the Corporation.* New York: Basic Books, 1977.

Levinson, D. J., Darrow, C. H., Klein, E. G., Levinson, E. B., and McKee, B. *The Seasons of a Man's Life.* New York: Knopf, 1978.

Pascarella, E. T. "Student–Faculty Informal Contact and College Outcomes." *Review of Educational Research,* 1980, 50 (4), 545–595.

Schuster, J. H. "Whatever Happened to *The* Faculty?" *Teaching Excellence,* 1992, 3 (5), 1–4.

Sheehy, G. *Passages: Predictable Crises of Adult Lives.* New York: Bantam Books, 1979.

Terrell, M. C., Hassell, R. K., and Duggar, M. "Mentoring Programs: A Blueprint for Growth and Academic Development." *NASPA Journal,* 1992, *29* (3), 199–205.

Terrell, M. C., and Wright, D. J. (eds.). *From Survival to Success: Promoting Minority Student Retention.* NASPA Monograph Series, no. 9. Washington, D. C.: National Association of Personnel Administration, 1988.

*MARIE A. WUNSCH is vice-chancellor for academic affairs at the University of Wisconsin Centers, Madison, Wisconsin.*

# PART ONE

# Perspectives on the Mentoring Process

*This chapter posits the view that mentoring programs should have a conceptual framework and a structure that ensures benefits to both individuals and the institution.*

# New Directions for Mentoring: An Organizational Development Perspective

*Marie A. Wunsch*

In "The Way We Live Now," a poignant narrative of her life and work in academe, Jane Tompkins (1992) describes her deep and disturbing sense of isolation, loneliness, and disconnection. As she describes her daily work life with students and colleagues what emerges is the discrepancy between her expectations for a close, interactive, and nurturing community and the reality of faculty, staff, and students autonomously busy with individual achievement and work. She longs for a "peaceable kingdom" where people devote time and resources to building supportive, mutually reinforcing human relations. Why, she asks, are human relations considered to be nonintellectual, too touchy-feely, and peripheral to an institution's main concerns? Tompkins's reflections reveal a condition that could be the result of growing institutional complexity, demographic changes in students and faculty, fiscal restraint, and increased competition for recognition and rewards, all of which impact the lives of academics. She concludes that not only does the conduct of academics affect the quality of their lives, but that the culture of the university itself militates against paying proper attention to the quality of its own *institutional* life.

Men and women enter institutions of higher education to pursue degrees and careers. Most come with high hopes and aspirations for achieving personal and professional growth within a nurturing community. How do these yearnings for personal relationships fit with the life of the institution? Must the institution attend to the quality of its culture by attending to the quality of life among its students and faculty? And what does all this have to do with the themes and content of this volume on mentoring in higher education? Like

NEW DIRECTIONS FOR TEACHING AND LEARNING, no. 57, Spring 1994 © Jossey-Bass Publishers

conversations about academic community, discussions of mentoring conjure up yearnings for a close, personal relationship that includes caring, teaching, and guiding between two individuals. Expectations abound that mentors and protégés will pair up naturally by mutual interest or attraction. Perceptions exist that the mentoring experience will happen informally and that mentors and protégés with good intentions will know what to do to identify growth issues, develop skills, and support development. Each will provide the other with a rich, reciprocal, and fulfilling relationship. In the absence of complaints, no wonder that so many people assume that mentoring is a good practice and that it works.

If this view of mentoring as the perfect collegial relationship is so widely held, why do few students and faculty engage in it? Why are so many potential mentees, especially women and minorities, isolated from mentoring? Why are mentees frequently disappointed in their mentors? Why are potential mentors reluctant to take on the role? Why don't we analyze the process of mentoring or assess its effectiveness? If mentoring is universally a positive process, why aren't mentoring programs a routine part of all student and faculty development programs?

After many years experience as a protégé, a mentor, and a director of mentoring programs, I am forced to agree with Jane Tompkins concerning life in the academy. At worst, what we expected never fully materializes and we are disappointed and unfulfilled. At best, we are still hopeful, but uneasy about scrutinizing what we believe to be an essentially personal relationship. Is it possible that we have missed one important component in the relationship—the institution itself? Can it be that in an academic institution, no relationship is purely personal, that every relationship is a political, institutional, and communal experience?

## Enlarging Dialogue on Mentoring

My proposition is that it is time to rethink mentoring in higher education, to construct a more holistic and organic model, to place it squarely in the context of the educational culture, and to confront the disconnection between individual and institutional goals. The bulk of the literature and research on mentoring comes from the corporate sector and reflects its values about developmental relationships and advancement. The academy has been too quick to adopt this foreign model at its own norm. It is time to move the academic mentoring concept and process from the informal and idiosyncratic to one with structure and reinforcement that ties together individual and institutional growth, and to go from vague good feelings about mentoring to the assessment and validation of its outcomes for individuals *and* their organizations.

Only when individual and institutional values and goals converge will individual growth and a sense of community evolve. When we liken the yearning for community with the desire for the mentoring relationship, we must not forget that organizational needs and benefits cannot be separated from the needs and benefits to individuals. Berquist (1992) argues that the "developmental culture" of the academic institution bridges the gap between the needs of the individual and the requirements of the institution itself. If the welfare of the individual and the organization are one and the same, their points of compatibility and mutual support must be found and nurtured. The concerns of individuals for growth, change, advancement, recognition, and support can be brought into harmony with the organizational goals for continuity, stability, growth, and community. Mentoring programs are a natural way to effect this symbiotic benefit.

## Expanding Personal to Organizational

The personal component of the mentoring process, whether it be faculty and students, senior and junior faculty, or senior and aspiring administrators, will always remain the essence of the experience. However, there are advantages to understanding that individual mentoring, whether we acknowledge it or not, is always done within the context and culture of an institution. The third party in the mentoring relationship is the academic organization itself. Classrooms and faculty offices are not autonomous units. They are constituted within the organization, such that much of what mentors and their protégés do responds to the expectations and limitations of the institution. Hunt and Michael (1983) also include such factors as the work environment, the social and financial support available to individuals for their growth and advancement, and structure as parts of the culture of an organization that affect the growth and progress of individuals. For a student, these aspects impact the successful completion of a degree. For faculty, they influence the quality of the academic career.

Mentoring, especially for women and minorities, may question the values and status quo of the institution (Sleeter, 1992). In order to provide information, guidance, and support, mentoring may challenge recruitment and retention policies, the content issues of the curriculum, and personal and institutional attitudes concerning achievement, advancement, and change. How mentoring is defined, structured, and supported reflects an organization's definition of who are the weaker and underdeveloped members of the community and who are those responsible for their nurture and development. Moreover, negative institutional consequences may result from the lack of mentoring. Women and minorities, often identified as underutilized and undersupported, require particular attention. Legal scrutiny, grievances about unequal advancement, low morale, low retention, and lessened productivity in the workplace are documented consequences of neglect (Noe, 1988).

## Emphasizing Institutional Benefits of Mentoring

Organizations really do benefit from mentoring programs. This truth should be fully acknowledged. The richest concept is that in which the institution by sponsoring and supporting mentoring becomes part of the mentoring triad with the mentors and their protégés. Developing young adults and junior professionals learn technical knowledge about the workings of an organization that helps them to cultivate a sense of control, competence, and effectiveness in their roles (Kram, 1983). Colleges and universities see this positive result played out in minority undergraduate student retention and achievement (Terrell and Wright, 1988). Graduate students gain advantages in job placement, research skills, and collaboration on publications that enhance the reputation of the department (Hunt and Michael, 1983). Junior faculty experience a smoother process in attaining promotion and tenure and remain in their positions longer (Johnsrud and Atwater, 1991). Mentoring can respond to the personal and career changes experienced by midcareer faculty (Schuster, Wheeler, and Associates, 1990).

Senior mentors benefit from mentoring relationships. Research on career phases shows that mentoring provides the generative and revitalization functions sought by older scholars and professionals (Blackburn, Chapman, and Cameron, 1981). Kram (1983) and Levinson, Darrow, Klein, Levinson, and McKee (1978) confirm that mentorship helps develop positive and secure self-image and helps integrate career and family responsibilities. Professionals who were mentored themselves are likely to become mentors of succeeding generations of professionals (Hunt and Michael, 1983). For each of these individual benefits there is a positive institutional consequence. In essence, the quality of an academic institution depends on the quality of the work and learning experiences of its faculty, staff, and students.

If mentoring students and faculty becomes a valued part of the human resource development commitment of colleges and universities, there is little question that the institutional life of academe can benefit. With positive mentoring programs, colleges and universities will benefit from and contribute to individual growth. The mentor-protégé-institution dynamic will meet both personal and communal needs. The kind of loneliness and isolation described by Tompkins and reported by minority students (Terrell and Wright, 1988; Pascarella and Terenzeni, 1978), by junior faculty (Boice, 1992), and by women (Noe, 1988; Johnsrud and Atwater, 1991) can be transformed into a mutual sense of obligation, loyalty, and fulfillment.

Jane Tompkins recognized that colleges and universities are made up of people who were attracted to a culture that prizes personal autonomy and independence. Yet they need to be a part of an enterprise larger than themselves and part of a group that shares a common purpose. Rethinking, revitalizing, and embracing mentoring as an individual and communal enterprise can fulfill these yearnings and needs.

# References

Berquist, W. H. *The Four Cultures of the Academy: Insights and Strategies for Improving Leadership in Collegiate Organizations.* San Francisco: Jossey-Bass, 1992.

Blackburn, R. T., Chapman, D., and Cameron, S. "Cloning in Academe; Mentoring and Academic Careers." *Research in Higher Education,* 1981, *15,* 315–327.

Boice, R. *The New Faculty Member: Supporting and Fostering Professional Development.* San Francisco: Jossey-Bass, 1992.

Hunt, D. M., and Michael, C. "Mentorship: A Training and Development Tool." *Academy of Management Review,* 1983, *8* (3), 475–485.

Johnsrud, L., and Atwater, C. *Barriers to Tenure: Faculty Cohorts, 1982–88.* Technical report, University of Hawaii, Honolulu, 1991.

Kram, M. K. "Phases of the Mentor Relationship." *Academy of Management Journal,* 1983, *26,* 608–625.

Levinson, D. J., Darrow, C. M., Klein, E. G., Levinson, E. B., and McKee, B. *The Seasons of a Man's Life.* New York: Knopf, 1978.

Noe, R. "Women and Mentoring: A Review and Research Agenda." *Academy of Management Review,* 1988, *13* (1), 65–78.

Pascarella, E. T., and Terenzeni, P. T. "Student–Faculty Informal Relationships and Freshman Year Education Outcomes." *Journal of Educational Research,* 1978, *71* (4), 183–189.

Schuster, J. H., Wheeler, D. W., and Associates. *Enhancing Faculty Careers: Strategies for Development and Renewal.* San Francisco: Jossey-Bass, 1990.

Sleeter, C. E. *Keepers of the American Dream: A Study of Faculty Development and Multicultural Education.* London: Falmer Press, 1992.

Terrell, M. C., and Wright, D. J. (eds.). *From Survival to Success: Promoting Minority Student Retention.* NASPA Monograph Series, no. 9. Washington, D.C.: National Association of Student Personnel Administrators, 1988.

Tompkins, J. "The Way We Live Now." *Change,* Nov.–Dec. 1992, pp. 13–19.

MARIE A. WUNSCH *is vice-chancellor for academic affairs at the University of Wisconsin Centers, Madison, Wisconsin.*

*A discussion of the impact of mentoring relationships in higher education with focus on the changing needs of adult mentors and protégés as they mature chronologically and professionally.*

# Mentoring: An Adult Developmental Perspective

*Mary L. Otto*

The concept of adults as changing—or developing—through their adult years was brought to public awareness and given credence by such books as Levinson, Darrow, Klein, Levinson, and McKee's *The Seasons of a Man's Life* (1978) and Erik Erikson's *Adulthood* (1978). The concept of adulthood and the needs of adults received little attention until World War II when considerable attention was focused on adult behavior (Hudson, 1991). Now adulthood as a time of change and even as a time of crisis is an accepted concept. During adulthood men and women refine their identities and determine their rightful place in the world. Adulthood, then, is not a state, but instead a process of learning and developing.

Because definitions of success or happiness differ, a successful career will have a differential impact on the lives of adults. For example, the business world defines success in terms of the bottom line (increased revenues), whereas the world of higher education weighs teaching, research, and writing to define success. Although this flexibility to define one's success offers freedom, it also carries great responsibility. There is no single picture of what adulthood looks like and therefore no single path for development throughout adulthood. Receiving guidance, advice, and support throughout adulthood can be extremely helpful when making choices. In higher education students have historically been mentored by faculty and administrators. In fact, graduate students can reasonably expect that faculty will assist them not only academically but personally and professionally. In addition to the faculty–student mentoring relationship, many faculty and administrators who are developing or changing the direction of their careers are also involved in mentoring relationships (Fallon, 1991). It is not just students who are plagued with questions about possible careers. Faculty face "how to be successful" questions related to tenure requirements, life-style/career combinations, advancement into administration, earning the respect of others, becoming a scholar, striving to be a good teacher, and many more issues. Because it is not possible to learn everything one needs to know by heeding other people's experiences, many life questions can only be answered through some combination of personal/professional experience and involvement within the system. More-experienced individuals can offer support and help less-experienced colleagues become part of the system so they can explore alternatives.

As higher education's complexities expand, so does the need for recognizing and formally defining mentoring relationships between adults in the workplace. People frequently attribute their professional successes to the influence of mentors or role models (Frey and Noller, 1986; Fagenson, 1988; Burke, McKeen, and McKenna, 1990). Kram (1985) suggests, in fact, that when asked about work, people consistently mention others who influenced them. The mentoring relationship is one that provides an environment that supports adults while they continue to learn and develop themselves. It is a supportive environment that allows closeness and distance and recognizes the similarity as well as the individuality of both the mentor and the protégé. Hudson (1991) points out that while there are many professionals who provide these mentoring services, most of them have not been trained to do so. Thus he advocates a specific model to train professionals to be adult mentors.

This chapter will discuss the impact of mentoring relationships between adults in higher education and focus particularly on the changing needs of adult mentors and protégés as they mature chronologically and professionally.

## Benefits of Mentoring

A mentoring relationship, unlike the relationship between a professor and a student, is most often made by choice and is based on mutual respect. A mentor provides practical, here-and-now advice (Bryant, 1984) which the protégé can use immediately to increase his or her effectiveness at work. A mentor differs from a sponsor, a person who has the influence to make sure his or her protégé is in the right place at the right time (Bryant, 1984). For example, a mentor might help his protégé prepare materials for advancement into an academic administrative position, whereas a sponsor would be in a position to ensure that the review committee interviewed her protégé for the position.

Mentors have achieved success and influence as defined by the institution and its faculty and staff. They know who the important people are, how to access resources, and how to influence policy decisions (Fagenson, 1988). Newcomers are likely to seek assistance from mentors they perceive as successful and/or powerful as well as potentially generative (Liden, 1985). Clearly, there are many extremely successful and powerful individuals who are not available to help others. They telegraph that message by avoiding contact with novices and by their unwillingness to share resources and experience. Likewise, some individuals may be very supportive, kind, and helpful, but are themselves not particularly successful, and therefore appear to be poor candidates for mentorship. While these individuals may become friends and supportive colleagues, they are not likely to be able to fulfill the requirements of a mentor.

Knox and McGovern (1988), in their study of female faculty members and students, reported that the six most important characteristics of a mentor are a willingness to share knowledge, honesty, competency, a willingness to allow growth, a willingness to give positive and critical feedback, and directness in dealings with the protégé. These characteristics are most likely to be found in middle-aged adults who have achieved some degree of professional and personal success and have the capacity for directing action in their own lives as well as the lives of others (Newman and Newman, 1991). Engaging in a mentoring relationship will assist the protégé's professional development and will celebrate the accomplishments of the mentor (Fleming, 1991).

Levinson, Darrow, Klein, Levinson, and McKee (1978) suggest that the role of the mentor for a young adult includes more than helping him or her achieve success at work. The mentor should "foster the young adult's development by believing in him [her], sharing the youthful Dream, giving it his blessing" (p. 99). While it seems obvious that the mentoring relationship is designed to benefit the protégé, it is also beneficial to the mentor. The mentor is able to influence the next generation through the mentoring relationship and therefore feels a sense of accomplishment as his or her protégé achieves success.

It is reasonable to assume that new faculty who are mentored may develop a stronger sense of commitment and allegiance to the profession (Wright and Wright, 1987) and perhaps even to the institution. Maintaining faculty loyalty may have been a concern in specific disciplines in the past, but faded as an issue in the 1970s and 1980s because a glut of available faculty for many academic disciplines diminished the need to cultivate and retain new faculty. More recently, however, with the decreasing numbers of people who are choosing careers in higher education, faculty and administrators are more concerned about promoting faculty loyalty and therefore may want to rethink their commitment to mentoring new professionals.

Mentors are important for both males and females, but may be essential for women (Roberts and Newton, 1987; Noe, 1988; Haynes, 1989; Ragins, 1989) who are seeking professional advancement. Mentors buffer discrimination and help women anticipate and overcome barriers. Because so many female faculty have had to overcome biases and prejudices to complete their doctorates, they may believe that they should work to achieve professional success without outside assistance. Thus, they may not recognize the importance of mentoring relationships or know to to access them without feeling compromised.

The number of female mentors remains small in higher education. A new male faculty member will automatically come into contact with a network of experienced male faculty, whereas a new female faculty member is not likely to find a fully developed network of female faculty. Although women do obtain mentors, they often have to wait for the mentor to step forward and initiate a relationship (Ragins and Cotton, 1991). Once they are in a mentoring relationship, women are more likely than men to stay longer in that relationship than is good for their careers (Collins, 1983).

## Destructive Elements of Mentoring

Mentors are attracted to protégés who demonstrate dedication, enthusiasm, intelligence, aggressiveness, and ambition in addition to other traits (Collins, 1983). Thus, mentors who themselves are influential and successful select protégés who have a high probability of success with the goal of guiding and directing their professional development. Mentoring relationships begin with the expectation that it will be mutually beneficial to the protégé and the mentor. However, the interpersonal and professional complexities of these relationships can result in negative as well as positive outcomes (Frey and Noller, 1986). While most mentoring relationships naturally develop into productive professional relationships and eventually into true lifelong friendships, some become counterproductive and negative.

Ultimately, all collegial mentoring relationships must change. The mentor and the protégé must become friends or colleagues of like or similar status if the protégé is successful. The difficulty of establishing this peer relationship is demonstrated by the tendency of doctoral students to continue to feel "like students" with their dissertation advisers and major professors even after they establish themselves as professional colleagues. The very personality traits (strength, competence, potential) that attract a mentor and protégé to each other also may underlie negative outcomes to the relationship.

A struggle for control may occur when a protégé decides to ignore or improvise upon advice from the mentor. A protégé also may develop faster than expected and may quickly surpass the mentor in skill and reputation, much to the mentor's dismay. Over time the protégé may begin to look for advice and guidance from other senior faculty and administrators, activity that can prompt a sense of loss in the mentor. As the protégé decreases dependency upon the mentor, the mentor may feel unappreciated and become resentful.

A mentor also may face personal and professional issues that may interfere with his or her ability to mentor. A middle-aged mentor may face a midlife crisis and be less available to provide support and guidance (Kram, 1985). In addition, a mentor may become professionally involved in work that distracts her/him from continuing to provide assistance. These personal and professional changes in the life of the mentor can be confusing to the protégé, often resulting in anger and resentment toward the individual mentor and the institution.

A new faculty member may feel betrayed not only by the mentor but by the institution—especially when the promise of a mentoring relationship was instrumental in his or her decision to accept the position. The junior faculty member may look for a new mentor at the same institution or may decide to move elsewhere to further his or her career. Although relationships are necessary to the quality of life and well being (Kram, 1985), like all other types of relationships, a mentoring relationship is affected by many dynamics that can have both positive and negative influences.

## Career Stages and the Mentoring Relationship

**Beginning Career.** Newman and Newman (1991) suggest that work is an important part of the development of a life-style and generally is part of the early adult developmental stage (age twenty-three to thirty). A majority of adults work throughout their life and spend more time in their work settings (Hudson, 1991) than they do in their homes. Thus it seems obvious that the work environment will have a major influence on the overall quality of life for most adults.

Careers, like individuals, develop in stages. Each stage has its specific needs and issues that need to be addressed by the protégé and mentor (Kram, 1983). The early career years, like the early adulthood years, are concerned with the development of a life-style apart from the family of origin (Levinson, Darrow, Klein, Levinson, and McKee, 1978; Kram, 1985). The protégé is concerned about developing competence, skill level, and a professional identity. The professor-mentor is challenged to treat the protégé as a novice colleague and not as a student. In fact, both the new and the experienced faculty members of a mentoring pair have to create a mentoring relationship rather than a student–teacher relationship.

The adult developmental stages of the mentor and protégé are likely to be different so that their personal as well as professional needs should be complementary. That is, the protégé needs to be nurtured and guided. The mentor is able to provide both nurturing and guidance because the later developmental stages of adulthood focus on generativity.

The older, more experienced mentor has the energy to support and guide the protégé because she/he has already developed a career. Newman and Newman (1991) describe *generativity* as a commitment to improving life conditions for the next generation and suggest that it conveys the depth of satisfaction with one's accomplishments as well as the realization that individual life does not continue forever. Acting as a mentor is a way to contribute to the next generation and to avoid stagnation.

New faculty are faced with many of the questions about their career and competencies that Kram (1985) identified as concerns in the corporate sector. In the early career years, questions arise about competency, identity, advancement, and commitment (Kram, 1985; Dreher and Ash, 1990). In most universities and colleges new faculty must integrate teaching, scholarship, and service to meet requirements for tenure review and promotion. Faculty must demonstrate, usually within six or seven years, their full potential to contribute to their discipline and to their institution. If they do not meet the tenure requirements, they are not able to remain at the institution. Thus new faculty are likely candidates for mentoring. They need to be guided in the development of a plan that will allow them to make the appropriate progress to gain tenure. At the same time, the mentor can help them understand their abilities, determine their strengths, and assist them in deciding if this is the right career path.

New faculty members, like novices in the corporate sector, must question their career choice. They must consider how well they fit with the demands of higher education, whether their values are consistent with those of the discipline and institution, and whether they can function without compromising themselves (Kram, 1985). They must discover an appropriate balance between career and family. Thus the mentor must help a novice professor examine not only his or her abilities and skills, but his or her professional and personal ideals and values. The mentor needs to provide accurate and timely feedback on the protégé's work, attitude, and behavior. The mentor may be one of the few individuals who is in a position to notice personal and professional life-style conflicts.

**Midcareer.** During the middle adult stage of life, many adults reassess their life-style, including their career choice, to evaluate and decide how to spend the rest of their life. In higher education, this evaluation may result in a change of direction, such as returning from academic administration to faculty status or moving into administration. Unlike the situation in many other fields, people in higher education can begin new careers at midlife.

In contrast to the individual in early career, the individual at midcareer is confronted with a unique set of developmental tasks (Kram, 1985) whether they are continuing, changing, or beginning their career. The midcareer individual has a substantial career and life history (Levinson, Darrow, Klein, Levinson, and McKee, 1978). Even if they are initiating a new direction, they know more about themselves and their career goals. An individual who decides to be more generative, for example, may begin a career in higher education so he or she can teach as a way of passing something on to the next generation.

At the midcareer stage, it is possible for the same person to be both a mentor and a protégé. The midcareer protégé may be changing positions or still advancing in his or her chosen career. He or she will still be concerned with issues of competence, identity, commitment, and advancement as these relate to the career (Kram, 1985). The contents of the questions will be part of their general reassessment of their lives. Questions at this stage (Kram, 1985) will include: How do I compare with my peers? What does it mean to be a "senior" faculty member? Do I still want to invest as much energy in my career? Some faculty may seek meaning in their career by examining new horizons within their academic discipline, perhaps by starting a new research project or a new book. Other faculty may decide it is time to move into administration and provide leadership to new and younger faculty. And, of course, some will decide to retire early or to begin new careers.

A mentor can assist with all of these decisions. The mentor role is to provide guidance and direction related to career and to life-style decisions. At this stage as well as in the early career stage, the protégé must make decisions related not only to competence but to his or her desired life-style. The life-style of an academic administrator is much different than the life-style of a full professor. Both require substantial commitment and competence, but administration is much more structured whereas faculty status is flexible. Administrators are likely to be evaluated according to their yearly activity and accomplishments rather than according to their overall teaching or scholarship. A mentor of a midcareer protégé, then, will be helping the protégé examine his or her accomplishments and make decisions about how he or she will continue his or her career. The mentor will usually be in his or her late career stage and will be changing from a more central role to one that is more consultative (Kram, 1985). One important way of contributing and maintaining positive influence in the late career stage is to mentor midcareer faculty. The mentor-protégé relationship between late career and midcareer faculty can be mutually beneficial, with both individuals gaining personally and professionally. The midcareer protégé also may serve as mentor to a new faculty member, thus creating through mentoring a true cycle of generativity.

## Stages of a Mentoring Relationship

Kram (1985), based on her work with the corporate sector, suggests that there are four phases to the mentoring relationship. While these stages have been modified here to fit the world of higher education, they follow the same pattern.

**Initiation Phase.** The mentoring relationship begins with the initiation phase during which the mentor and protégé establish a relationship. The initiation phase will usually exist through the first two years, leading up to the first review in the tenure and promotion process. During this time the mentor will provide concrete assistance by suggesting committee assignments, providing help with teaching, and discussing directions for scholarship. The mentoring function may be fulfilled by a department chair who has formal responsibility for initiating the new faculty member or it may develop naturally between the new faculty member and a senior faculty member.

Much of the interaction at this early stage will be focused on preparing for the first review and helping the new faculty member establish himself or herself with the rest of the faculty. The new faculty member will have to adjust to being "junior" and having limited status. During this stage the mentor-protégé interaction will be directed toward accomplishing specific work-related goals. The protégé must be receptive to advice and counsel from the mentor and the mentor must be sensitive to treating the protégé as a colleague and not as a graduate student.

**Cultivation Phase.** This phase of the mentor-protégé relationship will last until the protégé receives promotion and/or tenure, usually three to five years depending on the institution. During this time the mentor and the protégé will develop a more meaningful relationship based on personal and professional similarities. They may become involved in the same professional organizations, write manuscripts together, team-teach courses, and begin to develop a personal as well as a professional relationship.

The mentor will challenge the protégé to develop additional skills and assume additional professional responsibilities. The protégé will develop her/his potential by being challenged and encouraged as well as supported. There will be increasing opportunities for collegial interaction as the mentor and the protégé serve together on committees and engage in professional commitments. There also will be social interactions as they develop mutual friendships and professional relationships. Kram (1985) suggests that this phase of the mentoring relationship is the least uncertain and difficult of all the phases. It is during this time that the protégé experiences a positive sense of accomplishment and the mentor feels satisfied with her/his positive influence.

This phase ends when the protégé moves into "senior" status as a tenured faculty member.

**Separation Phase.** According to Kram (1985), this phase takes place after a significant change in the structural relationship. When the protégé joins the tenured faculty ranks, there is no longer a clear need for a mentor. Often the mentor and the protégé will spend some time apart since the protégé will likely receive a sabbatical and go away from the institution to complete some new scholarship. The mentor might begin a mentor relationship with another new faculty member or the mentor might be less available to mentor because she/he becomes involved in her or his own career issues.

While the separation phase involves some loss, it is also a time of positive change and movement. The protégé loses the sense of security provided by the mentor and the mentor loses direct influence over the protégé's career (Kram, 1985). At the same time the protégé feels excited about the new opportunities and the mentor feels a sense of pride. Since it is normal now to expect career changes throughout the life cycle (Hudson, 1991), both the mentor and the protégé may experience changes in their individual careers.

**Redefinition Phase.** In higher education the redefinition phase of the mentoring relationship will begin after the protégé and mentor have adjusted to the protégé's new status. Because sabbatical leaves are usually for one semester, this phase will often begin after one semester when the protégé returns as a tenured faculty member. The most common redefinition is for the mentorship to become a friendship. This is usually true whether both faculty stay at the same institution or one or both of them move elsewhere. They become colleagues with mutual respect for each other and they often share important personal as well as professional commitments.

## Summary

Mentor-protégé relationships develop and support new faculty in higher education. The mentoring relationship provides a mechanism to socialize and integrate new faculty and an opportunity for experienced faculty and administrators to influence and guide the next generation. The mentoring relationship, like other relationships, is subject to change over time and has the potential for positive as well as negative resolutions. The mentor and the protégé as well as the institution can benefit from a positive mentoring relationship.

## References

Bryant, G. *The Working Woman Report.* New York: Simon & Schuster, 1984.

Burke, R. J., McKeen, C. A., and McKenna, C. S. "Sex Differences and Cross-Sex Effects on Mentoring: Some Preliminary Data." *Psychological Reports,* 1990, *67* (3), 1011–1023.

Collins, N. W. *Professional Women and Their Mentors.* Englewood Cliffs, N.J.: Prentice Hall, 1983.

Dreher, G. F., and Ash, R. A. "A Comparative Study of Mentoring Among Men and Women in Managerial, Professional, and Technical Positions." *Journal of Applied Psychology,* 1990, *75* (5), 539–546.

Erickson, E. H. (ed.). *Adulthood.* New York: W. W. Morrow & Co., 1978.

Fagenson, E. A. "The Power of a Mentor: Protégé and Nonprotégés' Perceptions of Their Own Power in Organizations." *Group and Organization Studies,* 1988, *13* (2), 182–194.

Fallon, J. L. "Planning for the Year 2000: Women in Academe," *ACA Bulletin,* 1991, *76,* 32–39.

Fleming, K. A. "Mentoring: Is It the Key to Opening Doors for Women in Educational Administration?" *Education Canada,* 1991, *31* (3), 27–33.

Frey, B. A., and Noller, R. B. "Mentoring: A Promise for the Future." *Journal of Creative Behavior,* 1986, *20* (1), 49–51.

Haynes, K. S. *Women Managers in Human Services.* New York: Springer, 1989.

Hudson, F. M. *The Adult Years: Mastering the Art of Self-Renewal.* San Francisco: Jossey-Bass, 1991.

Knox, P. L., and McGovern, T. V. "Mentoring Women in Academia." *Teaching of Psychology,* 1988, *15* (1), 39–41.

Kram, K. E. "Phases of the Mentor Relationship." *Academy of Management Journal,* 1983, *23* (4), 608–625.

Kram, K. E. *Mentoring at Work.* Glenview, Ill.: Scott, Foresman, 1985.

Levinson, D. J., Darrow, C. N., Klein, E. B., Levinson, M. A., and McKee, B. *The Seasons of a Man's Life.* New York: Knopf, 1978.

Liden, R. C. "Female Perceptions of Female and Male Managerial Behavior." *Sex Roles,* 1985, *12,* 421–432.

Newman, B. M., and Newman, P. R. *Development Through Life: A Psychosocial Approach.* Pacific Grove, Calif.: Brooks/Cole, 1991.

Noe, R. A. "Women and Mentoring: A Review and Research Agenda." *Academy of Management Review,* 1988, *13* (1), 65–78.

Ragins, B. R. "Barriers to Mentoring: The Female Manager's Dilemma." *Human Relations,* 1989, *42* (1), 1–22.

Ragins, B. R., and Cotton, J. L. "Better Said Than Done: Gender Differences as Perceived Barriers to Gaining a Mentor." *Academy of Management Journal,* 1991, *34* (4), 939–951.
Roberts, P., and Newton, P. M. "Levinsonian Studies of Women's Adult Development." *Psychology and Aging,* 1987, *2* (2), 154–163.
Wright, C. A., and Wright, S. D. "The Role of Mentors in the Career Development of Young Professionals." *Family Relations Journal of Applied Family and Child Studies,* 1987, *36* (2), 204–208.

MARY L. OTTO *is professor of education in the Department of Counseling and special
assistant to the president at Oakland University, Rochester, Michigan.*

# PART TWO

# Case Studies and Program Models

*A comprehensive institutional mentoring program must consider all the components of the mentoring process to ensure personal and organizational outcomes.*

# Developing Mentoring Programs: Major Themes and Issues

*Marie A. Wunsch*

The second section of this volume illustrates "comprehensive" models of mentoring programs for a variety of participants in different kinds of academic institutions. These programs have considered the major issues in creating and implementing a program, such as defining mentoring within the institutional mission and goals, planning the mentoring process and selecting activities, developing a rationale for pairing mentors and protégés, securing adequate resources, and evaluating outcomes. For those beginning mentoring programs or enhancing existing ones, the research and literature provide a variety of perspectives on these major themes and issues.

## Defining Mentoring Within Institutional Needs and Goals

The literature on defining mentoring is drawn from a wide context: the popular press, corporate and trade journals, academic journals, dissertations, and descriptions of mentoring programs. While wide, it is neither deep nor very illuminating. There is actually no universally accepted definition of the roles and functions of mentoring. The popularization of mentoring as a "quick fix" for advancement in the workplace has blurred the definition, devalued the concept, and done little to advance the understanding of the process or the relationship. Higher education has been slow to define academic mentoring. Possibly the strongest perception is that mentoring is a form of teaching that goes on naturally between students and faculty and between junior and senior faculty colleagues. As is also the case with teaching, we are reluctant to define good mentoring and to evaluate its outcomes.

NEW DIRECTIONS FOR TEACHING AND LEARNING, no. 57, Spring 1994  © Jossey-Bass Publishers

When referring to a mentor different terms are used to differentiate the roles and functions of mentoring, but the terms are often used interchangeably. Some terms are more descriptive of adult development (graduate students, faculty, administrators) such as networking relationships (Swoboda and Millar, 1986), peer pals and guides (Shapiro, Haseltine & Rowe, 1978), coach and confidante (Bolton, 1980), or patrons and sponsors (Levinson, Darrow, Klein, Levinson, and McKee, 1978; Kanter, 1977; Kram, 1983; Zey, 1984). For students mentors are described as teacher, counselor, protector, cheerleader, and role model (Brown and DeCoster, 1983; Pascarella and Terenzini, 1978; Terrell, Hassell, and Duggar, 1992). When personal growth and academic learning rather than professional advancement is central to the mentor–student protégé relationship in academe (Merriam, 1983), the status-experience-age differentials become key defining factors. Philips (1979) describes the student–faculty relationship as one of master and pupil, sorcerer and apprentice, mentor and ward.

Recent literature is beginning to challenge some common terminology for mentors (godfather, rabbi, patron, master) as hierarchical, patronistic, exclusionary, elitist, and masculine. As such they may not reflect, nor support, the experiences of women and ethnic groups (Hunt and Michael, 1988; Paludi, Waite, Robertson, and Jones, 1988; McCormick and Titus, 1990).

Suffice it to say, those developing mentoring programs will get little conclusive guidance about definitions from the literature or from observing working programs. Acknowledging this limitation, program developers would do best by choosing a clear *operating definition* that reflects the needs of participants and the goals of mentoring within a particular institution. These goals can be as specific as teaching academic writing skills to graduate students or as complex as developing self-esteem in minority students or promoting advancement to tenure for female faculty members. By articulating the mentoring goals, it can be determined if mentors are to act as teachers, coaches, guides, or sponsors. Individual mentoring might also be supplemented by variations such as group or peer mentors. The operational definition should be, in turn, linked to the choice of mentoring activities and the assessment of outcomes.

## Moving from Informal to Planned Mentoring

Informal mentoring will continue to happen as it always has, for a fortunate few. Individual mentors and protégés will continue to choose one another and act as differently as human variety allows. However, when they agree to engage in a developmental relationship related to academic and career goals, they leave the realm of the personal and add the institutional. Defining, planning, and structuring activities within a goal and time frame is no longer a choice, but a necessity.

Who, then, is to plan and manage mentoring in an academic institution? If one member of the benefiting triad is the institution, it is the responsibility of that organization to coordinate and support formal programs. Since the 1980s planned, structured, or formal mentoring programs have increased in higher education especially for women and minorities who have had limited opportunity to engage in informal mentoring (Frierson, 1991; Gray, 1986; Sandler, 1993; McCormick and Titus, 1990; DeFour, 1991). While the recipients of mentoring may be different and the times require adjusted goals, the earliest record showed that mentoring began as a planned and structured process.

Let's take a historical digression. Mentor, the archetypal model in *The Odyssey,* planned his mentoring of Telemachus. While Odysseus asked Mentor to protect, advise, guide, and train his son during his absence, Mentor had specific mentoring goals. He was to teach the young prince the skills needed to become a warrior, leader of men, head of household, and future king. The son's journey to seek his father was a designed rite of passage into self-identity and adulthood. Telemachus's mentoring was neither informal nor haphazard and it was frequently supplemented by multiple mentors, including the goddess Athena, the ultimate mentor.

## Selecting and Training Mentors and Mentees

Targeted, structured programs with custom-designed goals and activities have the advantage of identifying all participants who can benefit from mentoring rather than relying on like people finding one another. Formal programs recognize that setting clear expectations for participants is essential, as is the training of both mentors and mentees to make the most effective use of the process.

Informal mentoring relies on natural selection, personality congruence, and happenstance. It usually evolves slowly over time as pairs learn to know and trust one another. Mentors who choose their protégés control the learning activities and their timing. Protégés tend to take a passive role, relying upon the experience, status, commitment, competence, and energy of the mentor to provide learning. That is not to say that benefits do not accrue from informal mentoring, but this system is slow, unsystematic, and unpredictable. The new direction for mentoring in higher education is systematic and comprehensive mentoring sponsored by the institution and available to all those who wish to engage in it.

Rather than simply viewing mentoring in terms of a relationship between two individuals, it needs to be conceptualized as a process. As a growth process it can be defined, planned, and evaluated. Several elements need to be considered: the time devoted to mentoring, the pairing of mentors and protégés, the training of participants, the selection of mentoring activities, and the life cycle of the process.

A time commitment on the part of both mentor and mentee appears to be a key ingredient. Pairs who do not meet regularly with specific goals in mind do not make progress or feel satisfied with the mentoring (Boice, 1992b; Wunsch and Johnsrud, 1992). The informal "Call me if you need me" or "Here is your mentor" models create more barriers than interaction.

Planned mentoring requires a rationale for choosing participants and pairing them. There are a variety of opinions on pairing or even whether assigned mentors are desirable. Should mentees be able to select their mentors from a pool of volunteers? Should they be of the same sex, from the same ethnic group, in the same academic discipline? How does one predict compatibility of partners? Should potential mentors be screened by the mentoring program? Are there required characteristics for good mentors? Are there predictors of successful mentees? The research on the results of pairing is limited. What exists does not support the superiority of any particular matching model based on gender, race, or age (Boice, 1992b), although mentees may have a personal preference for a mentor of a particular gender or ethnic background (DeFour, 1990; McCormick and Titus, 1990). One would also do well to assess the institutional mores and culture in doing cross-racial or cross-gender pairing, and be aware of the potential for sexual harassment or exploitation. Alleman, Cochron, Doverspike, and Newman (1982) conclude from their studies on pairing that character selection is not the key issue. In the final analysis, they conclude that mentoring is a set of behaviors that can be defined, learned, and practiced.

More than personal qualities, mentors require human relations skills such as attentive listening, assertiveness, feedback methods, and positive reinforcement techniques (Gray, 1986; Sandler, 1993). If academic career planning is the focus, mentors also need content knowledge of their discipline and understanding of the paths to advancement in their profession. Mentees can also be taught productive mentoring behavior. They need to know their own goals or be willing to identify and clarify them during the mentoring process. They need to have realistic expectations concerning what mentors can and cannot do. They need to be taught how to use the information and skills gained out of mentoring to advance their own development. In a comprehensive program, orientation and training are a key component in ensuring that participants understand the goals of the program and the effective use of the mentoring process.

Mentoring relationships have identifiable cycles (also described in various and interchangeable terms) that include periods of induction, development, and completion. Some thinking needs to be given to the length of the sponsored mentoring relationship and at what point it will end. Academic mentoring is bound further by academic timetables: students aim to complete a degree, faculty move from one rank to another. When time is urgent, planned mentoring becomes more essential to accomplish goals effectively and cumulatively.

## Obtaining Resources for Mentoring

In any institutional sponsored mentoring program, a basic question will be what resources are required? Which resources are most critical for the development and implementation stages? Who will be responsible for acquiring and managing resources? Is mentoring a cost-effective process for attaining goals?

Generally, mentoring programs are time-intensive and the most critical resource is a program coordinator. A structured program with a critical mass of participants requires a person with adequate time to plan, deliver, and monitor activities, even if these are limited to mentoring pairs. The initial program development phase may require a person responsible for doing a needs assessment, writing a master plan for mentoring, selecting and training mentors, selecting mentees, developing a network of patrons and advocates, and setting up an assessment mechanism. Even when the program matures, someone needs to devote constant attention to addressing the organizational and human concerns in keeping it functioning smoothly.

The choice of a coordinator should reflect the skills and experience required to fulfill the goals of a particular program. For student mentoring programs, coordinators can come from existing staff in student development, student affairs, counseling, or related units. Mentoring programs focusing on minority, special needs, or women students may come out of offices with these mandates. Some programs for both students and junior faculty are coordinated by individual academic departments; in these cases the key person would be the department chair or a designated senior faculty member. Most important, the coordinator should be identified with and situated in an existing unit connected with student or faculty development. The greatest risk for new mentoring programs is to place them in a temporary or peripheral unit without a support network or a financial base.

The question of compensation for mentors should depend on program goals and activities and the institutional incentive and reward culture. Mentors should have a clear agreement on what they are expected to do and the time involved. Compensation may consist of major monetary stipends or released time if the program requires time-intensive interaction with mentees or program presentations, or may take the form of rewards such as gifts of books and materials, computer time, or student help. The majority of mentors are faculty and staff volunteers who receive no compensation except the satisfaction of making a contribution.

Even so, the institutional community-building aspects of mentoring can be fortified by recognizing and rewarding volunteer mentors. Depending on the values and culture of the campus, recognition might take the form of letters of recognition from the president, dean, or significant administrator; recognition events or lunches; certificates; or T-shirts with program logos. Faculty should be able to include mentoring as part of their contribution to teaching or university service for the purposes of tenure and promotion. The program coordinator should be aware of what rewards have meaning for the mentors in a particular program.

In addition to the resource of a knowledgeable and visible coordinator, an effective program needs an identified place where participants can meet together, with the coordinator, or for activities, and where others can call to receive information about the program. If part of the program plan and goals, the cost of materials, speakers, staff and student help, program publicity and assessment should be factored into the financial plan for the program.

## Evaluating the Outcomes of Mentoring

If mentoring is to become more systematic, so must its assessment. Examining the current state of evaluating mentoring, several issues arise. The first goes back to the dilemma of defining mentoring: what is not consistently defined cannot be studied comparatively or longitudinally. The second is that informal mentoring occurs in a gradual, unsystematic fashion, making it difficult to study as a process (Boice, 1992). The third is that the definition and goals of mentoring must be linked to a plan for assessment of outcomes and the plan must be a part of the program design. One needs to ask the purpose for acquiring assessment data. Is it to gain feedback from participants as the mentoring relationship develops? Is it to discover the impacts of mentoring on the participant and institutional goals? Or is it to conduct formal research on some aspect of the mentoring?

Merriam (1983) evaluated the extent to which enthusiasm for mentoring can be substantiated by research and concluded that the literature on academic mentoring is biased in favor of the phenomenon. The literature is relatively unsophisticated, consisting mostly of testimonials, opinions on the benefits, and surveys of successful professionals who had mentors, or interviews recalling a mentoring relationship. Little is known about the impact of unsuccessful mentoring, or about mentoring models that do not pair individuals. Data-based research does not yet confirm definitively either the value of, nor the need for, mentoring. Yet none of this means mentoring should not be undertaken.

Formal research and assessment of mentoring programs is rare and fraught with methodological pitfalls. According to Carmin (1988), choosing a methodology for assessing mentoring is complicated not only by the definitional varieties, but by data collection relying primarily on ex post facto designs such as self-report and interviews, small sample size, data contaminated by subject response style and memory distortions, and idiosyncratic instrumentation for measuring results.

For those who wish to do research, as opposed to program assessment, the challenge will be to develop and use a combination of empirical methods that reflect the complexity of mentoring relationships (Wrightsman, 1981; Hill,

1982). Carmin (1988) recommends demographic questionnaires, specimen records of interaction, path analysis, and covariance structure analysis. But this level of evaluation will probably be of greater use to scholars and researchers than to program designers. Those engaged in faculty and student development would do well to have affiliate researchers who might contribute to the program by doing research and assessment as it progresses.

Traditional assessment methods will serve those who wish to use evaluation as a feedback from participants to improve the programs. Mentors and protégés can use a contract, a journal, or an activities report to articulate specific goals and implement activities that can be assessed for completion. Content analysis of mentoring narratives or journals can provide data on task completion, and self-reporting can provide data on development (Boice, 1992b; Wunsch, 1993). Satisfaction questionnaires, pre and postparticipant questionnaires and subject interviews (Johnsrud and Atwater, 1991; Wunsch, 1993) provide evidence of the impact of mentoring activities on individual participants.

Tracking the institutional impact of mentoring activities will require longitudinal studies tied to institutional goals. The retention of students or the tenure and promotion of faculty can be tracked, although it takes care to isolate the effects of mentoring from other factors. Program developers need to be aware of the kinds of information the institution needs and values. Systematic study of mentoring should be undertaken in order to more fully understand the implications of the relationship for the individual and the organization.

There will be continuing tension between those who view mentoring as an easy, informal, and personal activity between two individuals with good intentions and those who attempt to make it designed, structured, and institutionalized. However, if mentors, protégés, and institutions are to benefit fully, those who create and administer mentoring programs need to consider all the components as complex and interrelated.

## References

Alleman, E., Cochran, J., Doverspike, J., and Newman, I. "Enriching Mentoring Relationships." *Personnel and Guidance Journal*, 1984, *12*, 329–332.

Boice, R. *The New Faculty Member: Supporting and Fostering Professional Development*. San Francisco: Jossey-Bass, 1992a.

Boice, R. "Lessons Learned About Mentoring." In M. D. Sorcinelli (ed.), *Developing New and Junior Faculty*. New Directions in Teaching and Learning, no. 50. San Francisco: Jossey-Bass, 1992b.

Bolton, B. "A Conceptual Analysis of the Mentoring Relationship in the Career Development of Women." *Adult Education*, 1980, *30* (4), 195–207.

Brown, R. D., and DeCoster, D. A. (eds.). *MentoringTranscript Systems for Promoting Student Growth*. New Directions for Student Services, no. 19. San Francisco: Jossey-Bass, 1983.

Carmin, C. N. "Issues in Research on Mentoring: Definitional and Methodological." *International Journal of Mentoring*, 1988, *2* (2), 9–13.

DeFour, D. C. "Some Thoughts on Ethnic Minority Mentoring." *International Journal of Mentoring*, 1991, *4* (2), 14–17.

Frierson, H. T. "The Situation of Black Educational Researchers: Continuation of a Crisis." *Educational Researcher*, 1991, *19* (2), 12–17.

Gray, W. A. "Components for Developing a Successful Formalized Mentoring Program." In *Proceedings of the First International Conference on Mentoring, 1986*, vol. 2. Vancouver, Canada: International Association for Mentoring, 1986.

Hill, C. E. "Counseling Process Research: Philosophical and Methodological Dilemmas." *Counseling Psychologist*, 1982, *10* (4), 7–19.

Hunt, D. M., and Michael, C., "Mentorship: A Training and Development Tool." *Academy of Management Review*, 1983, *8* (3), 475–485.

Johnsrud, L., and Atwater, C. *Barriers to Tenure: Faculty Cohorts, 1982–88.* Technical report, University of Hawaii, Manoa, 1991.

Kanter, R. M. *Men and Women of the Corporation.* New York: Basic Books, 1977.

Kram, M. K. "Phases of the Mentor Relationship." *Academy of Management Journal*, 1983, *26*, 608–625.

Levinson, D. J., Darrow, C. M., Klein, E. G., Levinson, E. B., and McKee, B. *The Seasons of a Man's Life.* New York: Knopf, 1978.

McCormick, T., and Titus, P. "Mentoring: Giving Minority Women Tools for Advancement." *International Journal of Mentoring*, 1990, *4* (2), 31–37.

Merriam, S. "Mentors and Protégés: A Critical Review of the Literature." *Adult Development Quarterly*, 1983, *33* (3), 161–173.

Paludi, M. A., Waite, B., Robertson, R. H., and Jones L. "Mentors vs. Role Models: Toward a Clarification of Terms." *International Journal of Mentoring*, 1988, *2* (2), 20–25.

Pascarella, E. T., and Terenzeni, P. T. "Student–Faculty Informal Relationships and Freshman Year Educational Outcomes." *Journal of Educational Research*, 1978, *71* (4), 183–189.

Philips, G. M. "The Peculiar Intimacy of Graduate Study: A Conservative View." *Communication Education*, 1979, *28*, 339–345.

Sandler, B. "Women as Mentors: Myths and Commandments." *Chronicle of Higher Education*, Mar. 10, 1993, p. B3.

Shapiro, E. C., Haseltine, F. P., and Rowe, M. P. "Moving Up: Role Models, Mentors and the Patron System." *Sloan Management Review*, 1978, *19* (3), 51–58.

Swoboda, M. J., and Millar, S. B. "Mentoring-Networking: Career Strategy of Women in Academic Administration. *Journal of NAWDAC*, 1986, *49*, 8–13.

Terrell, M. C., Hassell, R. K., and Duggar, M. "Mentoring Programs: A Blueprint for Growth and Academic Development." *NASPA Journal*, 1992, *29* (3), 199–205.

Wrightsman, L. S. "Research Methodologies for Assessing Mentoring." Paper presented at the annual meeting of the American Psychological Association, Sept. 1981, Boston.

Wunsch, M. A. "Giving Structure to Experience: Mentoring Agreements as a Development Strategy for Women Faculty." In *Proceedings of the Sixth Annual Conference on Diversity in Mentoring, April 1993.* Kalamazoo: Western Michigan University, Sept. 1993.

Wunsch, M. A., and Johnsrud, L. K. "Breaking Barriers: Mentoring Junior Faculty Women." *To Improve the Academy*, 1992, *11*, 175–187.

Zey, M. G. *The Mentor Connection.* Homewood, Ill.: Dow-Jones Irwin, 1984.

*MARIE A. WUNSCH is vice-chancellor for academic affairs at the University of Wisconsin Centers, Madison, Wisconsin.*

*Mentoring minority students plays an important role in their acclimation to academic life and retention, but the search for conclusive evidence of what program design is most effective continues.*

# Mentoring Undergraduate Minority Students: An Overview, Survey, and Model Program

*Melvin C. Terrell, R. Kipp Hassell*

Mentoring appears to play an increasingly important role in meeting the needs of students who are most at risk of leaving college or university before graduation. First-generation college students, particularly minorities, drop out before graduation because of inexperience or frustration with academic settings. Many encounter rejection and cultural isolation. Others experience confusion about academic goals and how to attain them. Still others are discouraged by bureaucratic requirements or academic environments that are not "learner-friendly" (Fleming, 1984; Pascarella, 1980; Terrell and Wright, 1988; Tinto, 1987).

Formal mentoring programs are being designed to address the concerns of these students and to ensure them a quality academic experience (James, 1989; O'Brien, 1988; Paratore, 1984). By enlisting experienced college personnel to provide acculturation to academic life, institutions have sought to improve the campus climate, enhance the college experience, and increase the academic success of (1) first-generation college students trying to adapt to the life of a student, (2) students who must deal with differences between the culture of home and college, (3) students who face severe financial burdens, (4) students who experience blatant and subtle racism, and (5) students underprepared to take full responsibility for themselves and therefore vulnerable to

The authors acknowledge the contributions of Dr. Margaret Duggar, professor of English at Chicago State University, and Larry Brittan, Melvin C. Terrell's graduate assistant. The original publication of the study data described in this chapter appeared in *NASPA Journal*, 1992, *29* (3). With additions, it is reprinted here with permission of the National Association of Personnel Administrators.

uninformed decisions that carry negative consequences far into the future (Armstrong-West and de la Teja, 1988; James, 1989; O'Brien, 1988).

Students who interact frequently with faculty and other university personnel are more satisfied with their collegiate experience than those who do not "connect" with faculty and staff (Endo and Harpel, 1982; Pascarella, 1980; Pascarella and Terenzini, 1977). Effective mentoring increases a student's sense of integration and involvement by teaching interpersonal, social, intellectual, and communication skills. In this way, they learn how to form positive relationships. As a result, their attrition is usually avoided. Redmond (1990a) asserts that mentoring gives students the impression that their college or university is a place where faculty, staff, and administrators care about them. She further reports that underrepresented students are surprised and pleased with planned aggressive relationship-building efforts by faculty or mentoring program staff to help them persist to graduation. These actions are interpreted by these students as evidence of caring.

There is debate as to whether formal and informal mentoring are equivalent, or whether one is more beneficial than the other in bringing about student persistence to graduation and eventual career success. Chao, Walz, and Gardner (1991) found that mentees in informal mentoring relationships reported receiving more career-related support and developing higher levels of socialization within an institution than mentees in formal relationships. Yet the benefits of a personal coach and mentor seem so convincing that organizations have instituted formal mentorship programs to encourage these relationships and to maximize their benefits (Wilson and Elman, 1990).

Overall, there is little to be gained from debating the merits of formal versus informal mentoring since the two forms of mentoring appear to enhance one another. They are not or should not be considered mutually exclusive. In fact, a formal program that encourages the development of informal "side" relationships and even multiple mentors and peer relationships would only be strengthened.

Both informal and formal mentoring efforts can be directed by focusing on the target goals recommended by Redmond (1990b) for averting minority attrition. These are: (1) promoting greater student, faculty, and administrator contact, communication, and understanding; (2) creating a culturally valid psychosocial atmosphere; (3) intervening promptly when students have academic difficulties; and (4) encouraging the use of college or university resources designed to aid students with nonacademic problems.

Students appear to approach mentoring through two stages. First, they initially seek mentoring guidance because they do not have a strong sense of direction about their academic and career goals, and believe that they would benefit from the guidance provided by a mentor. Willingness to participate suggests that they have an awareness of their need for growth and interpersonal interaction. As they develop confidence and greater independence, they feel a diminishing need for mentoring. They seek to formulate their own goals and objectives and to take chances following through on their chosen direction.

Second, students again seek involvement in a mentoring relationship after clarifying and testing their sense of purpose. They come to realize the value of learning the strategies to avoid the pitfalls of a chosen academic or career path. As the mentee's sense of self-direction becomes stronger, he or she sees the merit in collaborating with a mentor to share insights and provocations to action. The mentee has learned to be autonomous and self-reliant, but also has a desire to interact and cooperate with his or her mentor and others.

However, a paradox arises concerning those who would be involved in a mentoring program. Rice and Brown (1990) found that the students most open to new relationships were those who were most likely to express interest in being a mentee. But this type of student actually has the lowest need for such growth. Apparently, those with the greater need for the nurturing and support mentoring can provide, for example shy, less assertive students with lower self-esteem, are less likely to seek enrollment in formal mentoring programs.

The question for program designers regarding this paradox, according to Rice and Brown (1990) is: "Should the focus be on students who already have relatively good interpersonal skills or should enrollment be balanced with students who may have a higher need but lower inclination to participate?" (p. 298). Aggressive formal outreach may be necessary to motivate those most at risk to become involved in a student mentoring program. Helping those most in need requires making arrangements to do what Hamilton and Hamilton (1992) describe as "building competence."

## Survey Research Identifies Program Models

Informal mentoring arrangements arrived at by mutual consent between mentors and students have long been perceived as significant for enhancing and nurturing students' collegiate experiences and professional career development. Since these relationships are idiosyncratic and highly personal, evaluating their actual outcomes has been difficult. The increasing use of formal, goal-directed mentoring programs for minority and high-risk students appears to be a comparatively recent phenomenon. Little information yet exists on the design and operation of such programs, and even less has been published regarding various program models or the components, goals, organizational structures, or other features of successful mentoring programs.

**Method.** The primary purpose of this study involved identifying and describing existing mentoring programs for undergraduate students in higher education. Special focus was placed on identifying the characteristics of programs and alternative models, including such variables as program objectives, target audiences, organizational structures, operational strategies, and performance and retention outcomes. The study's initial emphasis was to identify a pool of institutions known, or believed, to have established mentoring programs on their campuses.

The primary means for identifying such a pool was a mailing list of institutions whose representatives had attended or presented at the second annual conference on mentoring, whose theme was "Creating Success Through Caring," held at Western Michigan University in May 1989. Additional institutions were included through such approaches as networking, direct telephone inquiries, and referrals from colleagues. Ultimately, seventy institutions were surveyed using a questionnaire that we developed. The sample included a variety of institutional types: large publicly funded research institutions, small liberal arts colleges, church-affiliated institutions, and two-year community colleges. Thirty-eight institutions (53 percent) returned usable questionnaires.

Be advised that the results of this study—the patterns, trends, and approaches that emerged—cannot be used as indicators of national and regional trends or outcomes. Given the study's research method, and lack of randomization, the information synthesized in this report reflects nothing more than the pattern and characteristic approaches of the respondent institutions. Nevertheless, the results do add to the limited research on this topic. They provide information on the nature and scope of selected mentoring programs, and help to identify the kinds of research needed to assess the short- and long-term impact of such programs.

**Program Goals.** Most studies identify the importance of integration to the success of a mentoring program. Of the programs surveyed, by far the largest number were designed to promote retention, especially for minority students. In this respect, 81.6 percent of respondents identified minority retention as a program goal while 73.3 percent aimed at increasing academic performance. Other programs were designed for honors students, student leaders, and students with specific career interests.

The survey revealed that 45 percent of the programs were implemented for the freshman year only, while 53 percent provided services for the first year and beyond. The percentage of programs designed only for freshmen correlates closely with the percentages intended for students at risk because of high school grades (42 percent) and low ACT/SAT scores (40 percent). These programs were designed to ease the transition into college for vulnerable students. Over half of the programs, however, extended beyond the freshman year, indicating that continuing support was deemed valuable. Some programs offered mentoring to any student with special needs, including students with low grades, all first-generation college students, students on athletic scholarships, and some special interest groups (honors students, student leaders).

**Program Participants.** The most frequently targeted populations were minority groups: African Americans (63 percent), Hispanics (55 percent), Native Americans (40 percent), and "Others" (26 percent). Among those in the

Others category were all entering students, all students on academic probation, and all low-income students.

Most programs used a combination of faculty (73.7 percent), staff (52.6 percent), and peers (36.8 percent) as well as others, such as alumni (28.9 percent), to serve as mentors. Faculty were most commonly used, perhaps because of program concentration on academic survival. Individual meetings with mentors addressed academic matters (95 percent) and career paths (95 percent), as well as personal problems (87 percent). Most meetings also involved some level of social interaction (84 percent). Mentors met with students weekly (37 percent), biweekly (26 percent), or monthly (32 percent), while 5 percent of respondents indicated no pattern. Peers were often used in tutoring and orientation programs, in addition to big brother/big sister arrangements. Some programs required frequent small group meetings to discuss study skills, current problems, and academic progress. The programs also scheduled large group meetings: twice or more per term (45 percent), at least once per term (37 percent), or at least once per year (8 percent); 5 percent of respondents reported no pattern. The meetings were both informational (79 percent) and social (76 percent).

**Program Activities.** Considering the heavy emphasis on academic survival, it may seem surprising that student affairs divisions (47 percent) predominate in initiating and coordinating mentor programs more so than academic affairs (37.7 percent) or other areas, such as special programs and services (16 percent). The emphasis on developmental activities, however, may explain the reliance on student affairs. These activities involve both mentors and students. Most mentors were selected either by volunteering (68 percent) or by nomination (24 percent). Mentors were oriented by program directors (76 percent), staff (42 percent), faculty (24 percent), and the counseling department (32 percent). Orientation included discussion of program goals (92 percent), cross-cultural sensitivity (61 percent), elements of successful mentoring (87 percent), and student profiles (74 percent). Mentors and students were matched according to major (55 percent), personal or professional interest (58 percent), race (18 percent), sex (18 percent), and by random assignment (24 percent). Students' responsibilities for the mentoring relationship including making appointments with their mentors (71 percent), reporting difficulties (90 percent), reporting successes (76 percent), doing related reading (29 percent), getting study skills counseling (55 percent), and getting stress management counseling (45 percent). Nearly half (47 percent) of the programs had a full-time coordinator and 50 percent depended on state funding.

**Marketing.** Direct contact with students was by far the most common marketing technique. Most respondents agreed that effective promotion is important to a program's success. Many felt that students are sometimes uncertain about the potential value of participating in a mentoring program, at least when first approached. Most programs (92 percent) contacted students by direct mail. The approach used with the next highest frequency was informing the faculty of the program; this was done by 84 percent of the programs. Fifty-eight percent of respondent institutions disseminated brochures about their program. Forty-seven percent of the respondents reported sending letters to the parents of prospective students to make them aware of their mentoring program. Finally, 32 percent of the colleges and universities responding to the survey contacted and provided information about their mentoring program to feeder schools.

Significantly, nearly half the programs attempted to involve parents as well as their children. Some institutions reported resistance among faculty to instituting a program; most institutions found providing information to faculty important, both to procure support and to recruit mentors. Many respondents believed that an attractive brochure is important to building and maintaining support for a program.

Efforts directed to "institutionalize" the formal mentoring program would necessarily convince institutional constituencies of its importance beyond limited circles. This internal state of confidence in formal mentoring and a comprehensive external direct market approach involving a direct mail campaign to inform students and/or their parents of the program via a brochure and a market letter, as well as sending such information to feeder schools and faculty, could eventually lead to increased enrollments in mentorship programs.

**Retention Data.** While this study identifies the most common components of mentoring programs in a wide range of institutions, it offers little data that can be used to determine the ultimate success of the various programs in promoting retention to graduation and entry into mainstream life. Similarly, data are not available to determine which components are most effective. Since 63 percent of the programs surveyed had been in existence for five years or less, it is likely that not enough time has passed to allow for sufficient data collection to demonstrate their efficacy. However, some institutions are beginning to collect such data.

Only twelve (32 percent) of the respondents supplied information concerning percentages of students in mentoring programs who were retained. Retention rates ranged from 64 to 98 percent, with three institutions reporting a 75 percent retention rate and two reporting 90 percent. Only three of twelve respondents reported using control groups to determine program effectiveness.

In regards to pre- and posttesting, 58 percent of the institutions surveyed pretested applicants and 84 percent posttested their mentees. Further, 32 percent used instruments such as ACT and SAT scores to predict success, while 47 percent used grade point averages to assess the success of their program intervention. Attitude surveys going in were used by 34 percent of the schools, whereas 42 percent used such surveys after the program. Finally, a general questionnaire was used prior to intervention by 47 percent of the schools and after intervention by 68 percent of the schools.

Clearly, although mentoring programs have become an increasingly popular way to address retention and persistence, particularly among minority groups, there is not enough data available to prove their importance conclusively. So, while it is still difficult to obtain comparative program assessment data, highlighting working programs provides a mechanism for discussions on program development.

## Model Program

The Northeastern Illinois University Minority Student Mentoring Program was begun in the fall of 1989. Invitations to enroll were extended to all entering African-American and Hispanic freshmen. Of the 225 students who were eligible, 58 enrolled in the program that fall. Those who elected to participate did so in the very next fall term.

**Program Planning.** Planning began with a task force that surveyed the literature and existing programs to determine the need, the objectives, the rationale, and the guidelines for the campus program. All major phases were determined in advance, including participants, administration, major events, and evaluation. Over eighty faculty and staff (including administrators) volunteered to serve as mentors. Volunteers included the president, the provost, two vice presidents, and staff personnel, as well as faculty members.

The need and rationale for the program centers on the importance of providing minority students with a fair opportunity to succeed in higher education. Through the guidance and support of a mentor, a minority student is empowered to overcome previous discrimination, prior incomplete academic preparation, unfocused educational objectives, and therefore has a much better chance to persist to graduation.

The general aim of the program is to ensure a successful transition from high school to the university environment by providing caring and personalized support, encouragement, and assistance in making the adjustment. The following are the program's specific objectives:

1. To achieve a first-year retention rate of at least 80 percent.
2. To increase student persistence to graduation by the encouragement, support, and modeling of excellence and high standards by mentors.
3. To stimulate action-oriented career exploration and informed career decision making with an emphasis on increasing awareness and participation in majors and careers not traditionally selected or pursued by minorities.
4. To facilitate student awareness and utilization of university resources designed to enhance academic and psychosocial needs.
5. To enhance the campus environment by providing for positive interaction among students, faculty, and administrators which promote understanding, appreciation and validation of cultural diversity.

6. To strengthen and improve the supportive network for minority freshmen among peers, organizations, faculty, and support services.
7. To foster positive, nurturing, and caring relationships between mentors and students.
8. To stimulate and encourage increased contact between the student and his or her course instructors and academic advisers.
9. To compliment, enhance, and reinforce the efforts of the assigned academic adviser and other support services.
10. To promote ethical and moral development and a sense of commitment among students of service to other students and the community at large.
11. To increase students' college survival skills.

The guidelines for the program include an emphasis on mentors being available for sharing quality time with students and on joint participation of students and mentors in on- and off-campus events and social activities. Mentors were selected from among the faculty, administration, and professional staff because of their serious commitment to mentoring; their ability to listen actively, be empathetic, understanding, and nurturing; and their genuine interest in interacting with individuals of various backgrounds.

Mentors were also to acquaint students with the customs, resources, pathways, and awareness of institutional representatives of the university and professional world. Further, the mentor was to provide opportunities for the student who would observe and participate by shadowing the work of the mentor. Providing tutoring in academic areas and instruction in college survival skills and offering career advice were other ways the mentor helped a student. All in all, the mentor was expected to be an advocate for the student in his or her matriculation at the university.

Students and mentors attended separate orientations at which goals, objectives, and procedures were discussed by program coordinators and consultants. Mentoring was defined as both a tool for academic success and a human relationship between a student and a more experienced adult. Orientation also stressed cross-cultural sensitivity, and mentors were urged to present themselves as both friend and guide.

Based on a student's declared major, he or she was paired with a faculty member in that department. If a student had not declared a major, his or her interests were determined and matched with those of a mentor. Mentor and mentees were expected to remain together for at least a year and to confer at least four times per semester.

Mentors responded enthusiastically to the program, making efforts to keep in contact with their students, to check on academic programs, and to discuss areas of concern. The concluding event was an end-of-the-year luncheon at which outstanding academic achievements by students were recognized. Most mentors indicated a willingness and even an eagerness to be assigned an entering freshman in the next year's program. Many also planned to continue their associations with their mentee students. Students were similarly enthusiastic.

**Impact of Mentoring.** At the end of the second term, 92 percent of the participating students were still enrolled, while only 62 percent of the non-participating students still persisted. Of the fifty-three remaining students in the program at the end of the second term, only four (8 percent) were on academic probation, but of the seventy-six nonparticipating students still enrolled, twenty (26 percent) were on probation. Comparative studies of the two groups show no significant difference in ACT scores, indicating that at least with this measure academic aptitude was not a factor in the retention rates.

Comments by both students and mentors on the program's evaluation questionnaire distributed at the end-of-year luncheon were positive. The questionnaire required responses ("strongly agree," "agree," "disagree," "disagree strongly") to statements such as, "My mentor and I interacted well together," "I wish my mentor could have contacted me more often," "My overall experience in the Minority Student Mentorship Program has been good," "I will continue to contact my mentor," and "The Holiday Reception and Appreciation Luncheon were beneficial and more social get togethers should be scheduled in the future." One open-ended question was offered: "Please state whether you feel this was a valuable experience for you and if so *how?* If not, *why?*"

Sample student remarks included "I'm delighted with this program. I'm thankful to the teachers that have taken the time to spend with us" and "I have learned through this program that I can always go to someone for help and advice. Mentors observed, "It was a very valuable experience because it keeps me in personal touch with the student perspective," "I have come to realize that students' personal lives can be very challenging," and "You should include any student who needs the human touch of kindness and concern."

At this early stage the results exceed the 80 percent retention rate set as a goal for the program. However, this does not constitute conclusive evidence of the success of mentoring programs. This preliminary data does suggest that more extensive studies may confirm the positive outcomes of formal mentoring programs for high-risk students.

## Conclusion

Our initial and follow-up literature review, the survey research, subsequent analysis of statistical data, and our experience within an experimental campus mentoring program indicate that the formal mentoring relationship, a kind of "arranged marriage," does work over time.

While formal mentoring does not have the self-selecting quality of informal relations, it does establish a basis for matching students and mentors on such selection criteria as shared values, interests, goals, and attitudes in order to promote appropriate association. Further, it appears that informal relationships enhance the formal mentoring process in developing the individual student.

Effective formal mentoring is instrumental in helping minorities persist to graduation, although it is not yet clear from the research what particular mentoring program design is best for bringing about this end. Further studies are needed.

Nevertheless, we are optimistic about the future of minority mentorship programs in higher education. Mentorship programs will enhance the campus climate and foster minority student development on our college campuses. Consequently, our institutions will involve minority students more in their learning communities.

## References

Armstrong-West, S., and de la Teja, M. H. "Social and Psychological Factors Affect the Retention of Minority Students." In M. C. Terrell and D. J. Wright (eds.), *From Survival to Success: Promoting Minority Student Retention.* NASPA Monograph Series, no. 9. Washington, D.C.: National Association of Student Personnel Administrators, 1988.

Chao, G. T., Walz, P. M., and Gardner, P.D. *A Comparison of Informal Mentoring Relationships and Formal Mentorship Programs.* East Lansing: Department of Management, Michigan State University, 1991. (ED 333 784)

Endo, J. J., and Harpel, R. L. "The Effect of Student–Faculty Interaction on Students' Educational Outcomes." *Research in Higher Education,* 1982, *16* (2), 115–138.

Fleming, J. *Blacks in College: A Comparative Study of Students' Success in Black and in White Institutions.* San Francisco: Jossey-Bass, 1984.

Hamilton, S. J., and Hamilton, M. A. "Mentoring Programs: Promise and Paradox." *Phi Delta Kappan,* 1992, *73* (7), 546–550.

James, D. P. "Increasing Retention Rates of Black and Minority Students." *Mentoring International,* 1989, *3* (2), 34–39.

O'Brien, E. "Dr. Charles Willie Prescribes Mentoring Methodologies for Minorities." *Black Issues in Higher Education,* 1988, *5* (5), 15.

Paratore, J. "The Relationship Between Participation in Mentoring Programs and Developmental Growth and Persistence of Freshman Students at Southern Illinois University at Carbondale." Unpublished doctoral dissertation, Southern Illinois University, 1984.

Pascarella, E. T. "Student–Faculty Informal Contact and College Outcomes." *Review of Educational Research,* 1980, *50* (4), 545–595.

Pascarella, E. T., and Terenzini, P. T. "Patterns of Student–Faculty Informal Interaction Beyond the Classroom and Voluntary Freshman Attrition." *Journal of Higher Education,* 1977, *48* (5), 540–552.

Redmond, S. P. "Faculty/Student Mentoring to Improve Retention: Preliminary Findings of the California State University, Hayward Experience." *Annual Report,* California State University, Hayward, 1990a.

Redmond, S. P. "Mentoring and Cultural Diversity in Academic Settings." *American Behavioral Scientist,* 1990b, *34* (2), 188–200.

Rice, M. R., and Brown, R. D. "Developmental Factors Associated with Self-Perceptions of Mentoring Competence and Mentoring Needs." *Journal of College Student Development,* 1990, *31* (1), 293–299.

Terrell, M. C., and Wright, D. J. (eds.). *From Survival to Success: Promoting Minority Student Retention.* NASPA Monograph Series, no. 9. Washington, D. C.: National Association of Student Personnel Administrators, 1988.

Tinto, V. *Leaving College: Rethinking the Causes and Cures of Student Attrition.* Chicago: University of Chicago Press, 1987.

Wilson, J., and Elman, N. S. "Organizational Benefits of Mentoring." *Academy of Management Executives,* 1990, 4, 88–94.

MELVIN C. TERRELL *is vice president for student affairs and professor of counselor education at Northeastern Illinois University in Chicago.*

R. KIPP HASSELL *is dean of students at Northeastern Illinois University in Chicago.*

*Mentoring may prove to be the decisive intervention with high-risk entering students and requires the full resources of the campus and community.*

# Developing a Freshman Mentoring Program: A Small College Experience

*Keith B. Wilson*

Small private colleges with unique cultural contexts, special needs students, and limited resources face difficult challenges in implementing much-needed mentoring programs. The Freshman Mentoring Program at Brewton-Parker College is in its initial years of development and implementation. This chapter will discuss the attempt to meet the orientation and retention needs of at-risk students by drawing on members of the campus and the local community. While our program is still in its developmental stage, the lessons we have learned may be instructive to others considering similar programs.

Brewton-Parker College, located in rural south Georgia, was originally chartered as Union Baptist Institute in 1904. Accredited as a junior college in 1962, the college became an accredited four-year baccalaureate institution in 1986. There are few senior colleges in the southern half of the state of Georgia; the nearest to Brewton-Parker is sixty-five miles away. A major concern facing the institution is responding to the educational needs of low-income, academically at-risk students. Brewton-Parker primarily draws upon a thirteen-county area for its enrollment. This area ranks in the lower one-fourth of the state economically. Twenty-nine percent of the area's population lives below the federally recognized poverty level; 24 percent of the households have less than $10,000 annual income. The bleakness of the service area is further characterized by a high percentage of low-income single parents with limited educational backgrounds who are unemployed or are blue-collar workers.

The children of these families tend either to move away in search of better jobs or remain in the vicinity to do local farming, logging, or manufacturing work. The rural nature of the community means that potential students tend to follow tradition rather than seek new horizons through education.

NEW DIRECTIONS FOR TEACHING AND LEARNING, no. 57, Spring 1994 © Jossey-Bass Publishers

Approximately half the entering classes of Brewton-Parker in the past five years have not been retained. Academic failure, financial complications, and transfers to state institutions or other vocational training programs are the leading factors in attrition. Consequently, attrition and retention of freshman students are the primary concerns of the Brewton-Parker College administration and faculty. Mentoring for these students may be the most crucial intervention necessary for their success. Engaging members of the community, as well as college faculty and staff, in the mentoring process may provide the extra attention and role modeling that will make a difference to these students.

## Student Characteristics

In fall 1992 the college enrolled 1,924 residential, commuting, and incarcerated students. Forty-four percent of the college population enters the traditional day programs; 30 percent enters the evening programs offered at the main and seven satellite locations; and 26 percent are enrolled in programs offered at nine state and federal penal institutions.

Of the first-time freshmen enrolled in fall 1992, 59.9 percent were placed in the developmental studies program for remedial support prior to being enrolled in regular college courses. The college is an open admissions institution and the average combined SAT score is 788, lower than the national average of 899. Only 2 percent of the evening college program students are African-American males; 7 percent are African-American females. Nontraditional students aged twenty-four and over comprise 51 percent of the day student population, and of these 36 percent are Caucasian females.

As a group these nontraditional students face the difficulty of attaining an education while balancing work and family obligations. They may lack support from family members for their educational goals and must often weigh the economic investment in education against family needs. They generally have underdeveloped study skills, lack of time for school, and low self-esteem. They are apprehensive about being back in school and fear failure.

## Brewton-Parker College Freshman Mentoring Program

As evidenced by the low entrance scores and low retention rates over the past seven years, Brewton-Parker College is in need of a strategy to address the lack of success of the freshman population. High-risk students share the characteristics of all entering freshmen. These include getting acclimated and adjusted to academic life, meeting and interacting with peers, adjusting to academic stresses, setting goals and priorities for academic success, learning time-management strategies, developing self-esteem, and learning to be independent. In addition, the high-risk students lack the academic skills needed to progress in their courses of study. The college wanted a program to give these freshmen the added incentive to persist toward earning a baccalaureate degree.

We felt this could be achieved by matching freshmen with older adult mentors. The mentors act as role models, guides, and resource persons. While some students most need to learn about a future profession in order to make course and career choices, others need a supportive friend and guide on the campus or in the community. Many first-generation college students have misconceptions about what attitudes and skills are required to succeed in college. Since the majority of mentors have successfully completed postsecondary education, they can assist students who may not have parents who are experienced enough to guide them through the difficulties they will encounter as college students. Mentors who have weathered the educational process can identify resources to help the mentee adjust to college life. Even mentees with college-educated parents find that a mentor in their own field of study can be helpful in identifying or even providing job opportunities in the future.

The pool of prospective traditional students in this service area is diminishing. Brewton-Parker College is encouraging the increase of minority students and nontraditional women students. While this institution makes all efforts to address racial and ethnic issues, this geographical area's heritage of divisiveness contributes to a lack of support for minorities entering higher education. The Freshman Mentoring Program identified additional needs of minority and nontraditional women students, including the need for childcare, positive role models, and financial support. Currently the program does not provide childcare or financial aide, but role modeling through mentors is a high priority. Providing encouragement, guidance, and a sense of respect for minority and nontraditional women is an integral part of the program.

## Recruiting, Orienting, Matching, and Training Mentors

Developing a pool of prospective mentors is particularly challenging at a small, geographically remote campus. The Freshmen Mentoring Program must rely on willing volunteers from the campus faculty and staff, but not all are familiar with the concepts and skills of mentoring, nor do they yet see mentoring fitting in with their work load. The process of identifying mentors began by designating "resource leaders," persons active in community organizations who had professional status, contacts, and a reputation for service.

Recruiting mentors from the community was adapted as a strategy to enhance the reputation of the college in the community, as well as to enlarge the pool of volunteers. The college wants the community to be more directly involved in campus activities, to assist freshman students in adult interactions, and to provide vocational information that is difficult to obtain in a classroom setting. Once identified, resource leaders were asked to provide names of other individuals who could be recruited into the mentoring program. Some of the resource leaders themselves agreed to be mentors, as did members of the faculty and staff of the college.

**Orientation for Mentors.** The commitment and skills of the mentors are necessary for the success of the program. Before mentors were formally matched with mentees, they had an opportunity to become acquainted with the goals and requirements of the program. At an initial mentor orientation session, potential mentors had an opportunity to discuss the mentoring relationship and the kind of activities that would best meet program goals given the special students' needs. Understanding the characteristics of the freshmen is deemed to be of great importance. For example, mentees may display low academic achievement and low self-esteem. Many come from dysfunctional home environments or have no clear educational goals or support systems. Mentees may bring inexperience, lack of self-discipline, or unclear goals to the mentoring relationship. If a mentee misses an appointment or is not receptive to counsel, mentors have to be open minded enough to disassociate the mentee from the behavior. Mentors need to understand that negative behavior may manifest itself in order to test the mentor's sincerity and personal commitment to the relationship.

Mentors were urged to be persistent and not to allow initial negative behavior to undermine their efforts to build trust and to earn respect from the mentee. Mentors needed to understand the modeling effective adult behavior would be part of the mentoring process. This modeling would include acting responsively in relationships, developing good time management skills, and coping positively with conflict. In brief, mentors were asked to be developmental change agents for the students. The orientation session also emphasized the need to maintain continuity and a structured program in order to build rapport and to accomplish positive activities. The pairs would be expected to meet at least four times a month for the first quarter of enrollment.

**Matching Mentors and Mentees.** Potential mentors who chose to participate after the orientation session were matched by a set of priorities corresponding to program goals. Mentors completed a biographical sheet after the orientation listing their professional experience and interests, personal characteristics, and hobbies. Greatest emphasis was placed on vocational compatibility so that mentors could help the mentees develop around professional interests. Freshmen students frequently have misconceptions about the requirements and responsibilities of a profession. A mentee, for example, assigned to a practicing attorney could learn the routine and work of lawyers. Since care planning and guidance are important program goals, students have already received job opportunities through their mentors, thus enhancing their persistence in college and access to financial resources. In this way, matching meets both the personal needs of the students and the college's institutional need for retention of students. The pairs were also matched by race, religion, and gender. The cultural norms of Southeastern Georgia needed to be considered in this area, and all mentors accepted the pairing methods.

**Ongoing Mentor Training.** To provide support for the mentors the program instituted a Mentors Forum held each academic quarter. The forum is arranged so that mentors can communicate both negative and positive aspects of the mentoring experience. Community mentors had an opportunity to become familiar with each other and the campus staff and resources. To reinforce the goals of the program, the mentors discussed problems with the matches, evolved positive strategies to meet problems, and highlighted successful strategies. By creating a cohort of mentors engaged in a common goal, the Mentors Forum is benefiting the entire program.

## Recruiting, Orienting, and Matching Mentees

The college Admissions Office provided the names of students who had completed a file to enroll in the day program. All students were first-time matriculators. Both the mentoring program director and the president of the college sent letters of invitation to all these students, asking them to participate, to establish the credibility of the program. The prospective mentees were invited to an orientation session during freshmen orientation week. During a two-hour session they were informed about the program and the potential benefits that could come from a mentoring relationship. Mentees were told that mentors could help them get acclimated to college, teach them skills for time management and adult interaction, could increase their level of independence, and would provide vocational development.

The mentees were told that they would be expected to meet with their mentors four times a month for the first quarter and that they were to take the initiative in contacting their mentor. The orientation session also included practical information and role playing about establishing rapport, building trust, and tying mentoring activities to wider academic goals. The potential to make vocational contacts and receive job opportunities was a high motivation for students to participate.

In the first year of the program fifty-eight students requested mentors and fifty-four were matched. Sixty-four percent of the freshman class participated in the program. Sixty-one percent of the mentors were from faculty and staff; 39 percent were from the community. The majority of pairs were in human services disciplines and work units. Caucasian students constituted 61 percent of the mentees, and 64 percent of the mentors were Caucasian. African-American students comprised 27 percent of the mentees, and African-Americans constituted 35 percent of the mentors.

After one quarter only eight of the fifty-eight mentees have dropped out of school. This is an 88 percent retention rate for mentees, compared with a 53 percent retention rate for all freshmen. While there is still need for more formal and long-term assessment measures, the preliminary data on retention and student satisfaction indicate that the program is successful in its retention goal.

## Conclusions

It is apparent from the emphasis on mentoring programs for students developed across the different sectors of higher education that mentoring does work to encourage and support students. For high-risk and minority students it may be a significant intervention. While the Freshman Mentoring Program at Brewton-Parker College is still developing and is similar to efforts in other institutions, we have made special efforts to tailor the program to the special needs of our particular high-risk student body in an open admissions institution. Drawing on mentors from the community as well as campus faculty and staff serves the wider agenda of securing community involvement in the success of students while also providing the traditional benefits of individual mentoring.

In assessing the developmental stage of the program, we have identified several areas that will be considered further as the program develops.

*Administrative support is crucial.* To ensure an effective organizational structure, financial resources, and adequate program coordination, senior administrators must be involved as sponsors and advocates of the program. If the community at large is to be drawn into the mentoring program, this element of contact and support must be highly visible.

*Mentors must be trained to mentor.* The nature of mentoring is complex and requires special attitudes and skills to be effective. Volunteers may have humane motives and a strong commitment to help, but they need context and techniques to perform effectively. We plan to spend at least eight additional hours working with the mentors during an extended orientation period. The sessions will emphasize the implications of the student characteristics on the mentoring process, the need for open communication and clear understanding of program goals, and the necessity for time commitments and structured activities.

*Mentees must be trained to use the program effectively.* Taking an active part in their own development, including meeting with mentors, completing update forms, and providing feedback on the mentoring process, is an essential discipline for the growth experience. Mentoring cannot be a passive experience for the mentees. Thos joining the program need to make clear commitments in tems of the time and energy it takes to benefit from structured mentoring activites.

*Short- and long-term assessment is necessary.* At the onset of a program it is easy to count numbers of students retained in college, but it is more difficult to chart developmental growth due to the mentoring process. If more self-esteem, greater academic success, and clear academic planning are also goals of the program, it will take a longer mentoring record and more sophisticated assessment to validate achievements of mentoring. The program does plan to acquire more quantitative data as well as qualitative data from the mentor and mentee feedback on the mentoring process over time. Participant self-assessment will also allow for program refinement past the initial year.

*KEITH B. WILSON is director of counseling services and adjunct professor of psychology at Brewton-Parker College, Mount Vernon, Georgia.*

*This chapter discusses a mentoring program designed to foster a culture that values and enables the success of faculty women.*

# Enabling the Success of Junior Faculty Women Through Mentoring

*Linda K. Johnsrud*

The title of this chapter prompts two obvious questions: why faculty *women*? and why *mentoring*? The answer to the first question is straightforward. Increasing evidence indicates that women's experience in colleges and universities is strikingly different from that of their male peers. National data demonstrate that women faculty tend to be promoted and tenured more slowly than their male peers and are more likely to leave an institution prior to gaining tenure (Finkelstein, 1984; Menges and Exum, 1983; Rausch, Ortiz, Douthitt, and Reed, 1989). The feelings of isolation, loneliness, and disconnectedness experienced by women faculty are well documented (Bourguignon and others, 1987; Johnsrud and Atwater, 1991a; Olsen, Maple, and Stage, 1991; Yoder, 1985). Given the low numbers of women in faculty positions, many individual women are the first and/or the only women in their departments. Women are not as well integrated into departmental or institutional networks (Eveslage, Stonewater, and Dingerson, 1987; Kaufman, 1978); they report more difficulties in relationships with departmental chairs and colleagues (Johnsrud and Atwater, 1991a); and they describe themselves as "outsiders," feeling that they do not belong (Aisenberg and Harrington, 1988). It is evident that if colleges and universities wish to retain and advance women faculty, they must find ways to address the professional isolation women faculty so typically experience, particularly in their early career years.

The answer to the second question—Why *mentoring*?—may seem equally as obvious but does need to be expressed with some caution. Essentially, mentoring for faculty means coupling those who have been successful in achieving tenure and promotion with those aspiring to reach these traditional milestones of academic achievement. Popular understanding suggests that

NEW DIRECTIONS FOR TEACHING AND LEARNING, no. 57, Spring 1994 © Jossey-Bass Publishers

being mentored is a sure ticket to success. In reality, we know very little about the long-term outcomes of mentoring relationships—little empirical work has been generated on this topic. Moreover, mentoring programs are not without their critics. Some would argue that the success of junior women faculty should not be the responsibility of senior faculty, particularly senior women who tend to be overworked as it is. Some caution against building dependent relationships. Others fear exploitation. Still other critics believe that mentoring programs serve to socialize, and ultimately, to co-opt junior women to the system rather than promoting institutional change. The purpose of this chapter is to describe the creation of a mentoring program for junior women faculty that includes systematic assessment of the impact of the program upon individual participants as well as its impact upon the culture of the university. The following discussion highlights a successful three-year program at the University of Hawaii for the mentoring of junior faculty women.[1]

## Beginnings

Many campuses have come to realize that the recruitment of women faculty is only the first step in a long process. If the goal of this process is to increase the proportion of women holding tenured faculty positions, then specific efforts to retain qualified women are needed. Mentoring is often mentioned as a means to enable the success of individual women faculty but rarely is a mentoring program for women institutionalized. Launching a program that has the potential to become an ongoing activity requires resources—and securing resources requires justification. Thus, the women faculty mentoring program at the University of Hawaii began with considerable attention to available data—both national and institutional—as well as a needs assessment.

The University of Hawaii study on *Barriers to Retention and Tenure: The Experiences of Faculty Cohorts, 1982-88* (Johnsrud and Atwater, 1991a) informed the evolution of the mentoring program. The study included 325 faculty who entered tenure-track positions, including 93 who left the institution, 127 who were still probationers, and 105 who had received tenure. The study concluded that women experienced their academic careers differently than did their male peers. Women in the study left their tenure-track positions at a rate significantly higher than did men (women comprised 34.1 percent of the population, but 45.2 percent of the leavers). Women faculty reported a greater lack of access to institutional resources and support, more isolation, more tenure pressure, greater workload imbalance, more stressful relations with colleagues and department chairs, and greater discrimination. Their expressed need for mentoring was widespread.

Before beginning the mentoring program, an institutional needs assessment was conducted surveying all senior faculty women (tenured associate and full professors) and all probationary women faculty (assistant professors), as well as a cohort of new women entering the university in the fall. Junior women identified a variety of needs in the areas of career planning, teaching development, research support, dual career issues, orientation to a multicultural campus, and personal adjustment issues. Senior women identified areas in which they had experience and areas in which they had expertise or interest in mentoring.

Grounding a mentoring program in institutional data provides information not only for justifying resources but also for the planning and implementation of the program. Moreover, an initial needs assessment lays the foundation for an ongoing assessment of outcomes.

## Structure

A mentoring program must be housed in a stable supportive unit with adequate resources and leadership committed to making the program a success. At the University of Hawaii, the Office of Faculty Development and Academic Support is charged with sponsoring developmental programs for all new faculty (new faculty orientation, teaching development seminars, workshops on institutional resources, travel monies, and curriculum development grants) as a retention strategy as well as for professional growth. The mentoring program for junior women faculty was a natural addition to its agenda. Placing responsibility for the program with a senior administrator and in an established program for serving faculty made it clear that mentoring was seen by the administration as a sanctioned and credible part of an integrated effort to retain new faculty. The program was supported by an initial $10,000 grant to cover staff support, materials, and small stipends for the mentors.

## Goals

In this program, mentoring is considered to be one part of a long-range integrated career development strategy, so that multiple activities are directed toward fostering career growth from the time a women faculty member enters the institution through her tenure and subsequent promotions. Although the pairing of colleagues is the primary focus of this discussion, it is important to note that the pairing is supported by training, large and small group meetings, and social activities. In general, the program has three primary emphases:

First, *entry-level survival needs are the priority in the first year.* Each academic department has a particular sociopolitical culture with its own implicit and explicit policies, norms, and interpersonal expectations. Moreover, the university as a whole has a culture that will affect the individual's academic career. As new faculty enter these arenas, they require access to information to function as accepted peers and professionals. Research has indicated that critical incidents in the first year, sometimes even in the first semester, often determine success or failure, retention or attrition (Boice, 1992). Mentors can respond to their mentees' first impressions and interpret their initial experiences to help new-comers understand and cope with their new surroundings. Mentors can help new faculty find the needed balance between preserving autonomy and achieving integration into the scholarly community of their department and institution. They can also provide institutional information on services, benefits, and intramural monies for teaching, travel, or research, as well as act as advocates for the new faculty. For this reason, newcomers were paired with a mentor from outside the home department, but in a cognate discipline or from the same college, who had extensive knowledge of campus routines and rituals.

Second, *the groundwork for career development and advancement must be laid early*. In the press of first-year orientation and adjustment, new faculty members seldom seem to see themselves planning an academic career. Yet most institutions almost immediately require some assessment for contract renewal, and the results begin to affect retention decisions on each side. Beyond their concern with first-year survival, new faculty must quickly learn the particular contributions they are expected to make to attain tenure and promotion. Mentors must make a special point of advising mentees about the importance of understanding review criteria and the evaluation process from early in the first year. Data such as student and peer evaluations, research proposals, and letters of support need to be acquired early for constructing the history of achievement necessary for the tenure dossier.

Third, *sociopsychological needs contribute to the sense of belonging*. All faculty should expect a campus climate that offers full collegiality and respect for individuality. Nonetheless, some women faculty experience hostility in their departments, and others experience benign neglect. The human connection that mentors provide can be vital to a socially and intellectually isolated junior woman. Being included in social gatherings, having a regular lunch partner, or even getting friendly telephone calls can make a difference in the quality of life experienced by the newcomer. Mentors can also serve as guides and models in helping to develop the skills needed to cope with less-than-congenial relationships, as well as in suggesting ways to influence the climate of the department so that women are included and respected as colleagues.

## Pairings

Senior and junior colleagues were paired by the program advisory committee on the basis of information supplied about career needs in the initial assessment survey. If voluntary data were included on life-style issues, every attempt was made to match women with similar backgrounds and family situations (for example, dual-career couples or mothers of small children). All mentors were senior, tenured women faculty, and each was from a related discipline outside the mentees' home department. At this time in the University of Hawaii program, only senior faculty women have been asked to serve as mentors. Although many male faculty could be of immense assistance to younger female faculty, women are paired on the assumption that they can most effectively facilitate the networking of women faculty, provide role models for successful careers, and convey the lessons of their own experiences. Pairing outside the home department provides a more neutral adviser while the new faculty members are gaining insight into the politics and practices of the department. Outside mentors are often able to be objective advocates for the new women with senior colleagues or the department chair in a way that might not have been possible if the woman mentor came from within the same department.

During the first year of our mentoring program there were thirty-four colleague pairs from twenty-seven different departments. Particular attention was given to pairing new women who were the first or only females in their departments. Two such women in the natural sciences had two mentors to ensure additional advice on grant and research development, matters of particular concern in the sciences. Mentees were also encouraged to identify other mentors, male or female, within their own departments who might help them to work on more specific aspects of colleague relations and expectations in the department.

In the second year another eighteen pairs were added, and in the third year another twenty-eight pairs were initiated. Simultaneously, three mentoring groups were set up to accommodate women faculty whose primary responsibilities were other than teaching and research (for example, librarians, student support specialists, non-tenure-track foreign language instructors). In this model, mentors and mentees work together in groups and evolve a general agreement on the areas in which they wish to focus their discussions and activities.

## Training

A number of mentors expressed concern about their ability to carry on a mentoring relationship and about the elusiveness of the process itself. Many had not had mentors themselves or had never engaged in mentoring activities. At the same time, others were uneasy about structuring a process that they felt was personal and informal. Mentors agreed to meet once a month as a group with the program coordinator to discuss the mentoring process, to identify more resources or persons to support their mentees, and to identify common professional or institutional problems encountered by new faculty. The program coordinator contributed articles and research on mentoring, as well as information on institutional resources that supported mentoring. Mentors often described "critical incidents" and asked for suggestions from other mentors on how to best guide their mentee. The year-end assessment indicated that the mentors thought that this structure helped considerably in terms of focusing activities. The mentors also reported benefiting from interaction with other senior colleagues, some of whom they had not met before entering the program (Johnsrud and Atwater, 1991b).

## Activities

Each colleague pair agreed to complete a written agreement in which they detailed how often they would meet and what specific activities they would pursue based on the interests and needs of the mentee. The written agreement was designed to be a tool for two persons who do not know one another to quickly begin the process of developing a working relationship. Discussing specific professional development issues forced the junior colleague to conceptualize and detail her own career needs and to identify strategies to address those needs. Guidelines for the written agreement were loose; the only requirement was that a plan be developed by mutual agreement of the pair. Otherwise, they were free to make individual decisions on time commitments and the number and kinds of activities. Although there was some resistance to even this amount of structure, those who established clear objectives and maintained the time commitment to meet regularly reported the most productive and personally satisfying experiences. Half the pairs in the group met at least once a month, and the other half met about twice a month. Over half the pairs also kept in touch by telephone and electronic mail, or met to participate in a professional or social activity in addition to their mentoring meeting.

The mentees also met once a month as a group with the program coordinator to analyze their own experiences, to develop personal contacts and professional relationships within the cohort, to identify common problems, and to detail actual strategies used to address critical issues. Close association with their peer cohort confirmed that their issues were common adjustment patterns of new faculty and eased some of the isolation and stress of "going it alone" as a newcomer. A number of research and writing collaborations were formed, and some social activities were planned by single women. In the second year a group of minority women in the program formed a focus group to meet separately on occasion to discuss their experiences as minority women faculty.

Some topics of common interest could be handled most effectively in a large-group format. These became the basis for two-hour seminars presented by individual experts or panels of women faculty. The advantage of this open format was that all women on campus, not only those in the mentoring program, could be invited. Some of the topics addressed were using academic writing groups, planning for tenure from the first year, time management and balancing priorities, and developing a scholarly agenda; a workshop on how to obtain intramural funds for research, travel, and career development was also included. Mentors frequently came to these sessions with their mentees, thus providing another opportunity for interaction as well as a richer mix of expertise on the topic.

Because many junior faculty report social and intellectual isolation and difficulty meeting faculty from other departments, a series of informal social events were offered to women faculty. There was an opening luncheon followed by monthly brown-bag lunches open to all faculty women. These provided an opportunity to develop relationships on a more personal basis and in a relaxed environment.

## Assessment

Two objectives shaped the assessment: to provide immediate information to guide the planning of activities and training, and to establish baseline data for an ongoing program. Thus, the assessment proceeded in three stage: (1) a preprogram survey, (2) a postprogram survey, and (3) individual interviews after each academic year.

The preprogram assessment was intended to identify the barriers experienced by women faculty early in their academic careers, to provide information on the expectations of the participants, and to guide the activities for the year. The first-year results indicated that senior and junior women perceived common potential barriers regarding the early years of their experience in the academy; nonetheless, there were important differences that made a difference in the program (Johnsrud and Wunsch, 1991a). For example, one barrier that senior women did not anticipate to be of high priority for junior women was writing. The writing issue, including finding time to write, editing, and the motivation to write, was the highest ranked barrier perceived by junior women. Senior women anticipated that productivity and the tenure clock would be major concerns, which may reflect their longer view of the tenure process. But junior women's concern was the first step: writing. Their emphasis on writing itself suggested the need for a specific response to this problem. As a result, a group session on the effectiveness of writing groups was sponsored for all interested junior faculty women, and several writing groups were initiated.

At the end of each spring semester, a postprogram survey was used to examine any changes in perceptions of the barriers to success, and to assess the success of the colleague pairing program. Not surprisingly, the results indicated that the senior and junior women's perceptions moved closer together over the course of the program (Johnsrud and Wunsch, 1991b). One concern, however, had implications for future planning. Junior faculty indicated that their "career goals" continued to be a major concern—one that was not perceived as a significant issue by senior faculty. It appeared that junior faculty was questioning their career choices or their futures more than senior faculty had realized. The following fall this topic was emphasized and addressed in a two-hour seminar.

Individual interviews were conducted at the end of each year with both members of the colleague pair. An open-ended interview guide was developed to elicit comments about each individual's experience in the mentor–mentee relationship and the program in general, including suggestions for change. Interviews were conducted one-on-one and were audiotaped. Analysis of the transcribed interviews indicated that the support for the mentoring program by all participants interviewed was overwhelmingly positive. Even in the few cases in which the individuals had less-than-satisfactory personal relationships with their particular mentor or mentee, they expressed strong support for the program as a whole.

Relationships were seen as most helpful in the areas of departmental and institutional politics, and the tenure process. Generally, it was perceived that relationships worked well when the mentor served as an active listener facilitating the mentee's own problem-solving abilities, offered emotional support and encouragement in professional and personal matters, and suggested strategies for dealing with department relations and the tenure clock. Mentors were able to provide a new perspective on institutional politics and procedures that helped extend the mentee's view and understanding of the institution. The mentoring relationship was also seen as helpful in dealing with the tenure clock, particularly in the balancing of teaching, research, and service.

For the most part, criticisms of the mentoring program are rare and idiosyncratic. Some like structure; some don't. Some prefer one-to-one relationships; others like groups. Concern was expressed regarding confidentiality, but it does not seem to be a problem. Time seems to be the major barrier to quality relationships, and even in that regard the commitment of the participants seems to supersede the time constraints.

Yearly assessments of the mentoring program proved to be useful for program planning and training, as well as for the long-term development of the program. A long-range assessment mechanism will be a longitudinal study of the cohorts as they proceed from entrance into the university through the completion of the tenure process. It will be important to identify changes in the needs and perceptions of participants as they move through the tenure process.

## Institutional Impact

There are a number of ways in which the success of a mentoring program can be measured. On the individual level, it is hoped that women faculty will succeed in their bid for tenure and advancement. On the institutional level, it is hoped that the program will be made a permanent part of an ongoing commitment to the retention of women faculty. Perhaps most importantly, by enabling women faculty to succeed and secure their positions in the academy, its climate and culture will become more conducive to the work and lives of women. Even three years into a program is too early to judge, but the signs are promising.

The junior women faculty mentoring program was named one of the president's initiatives, assuring further visibility and resources. The continuation of the program is enhanced by being included in crucial planning documents such as the campus academic development plan and the affirmative action plan, and in budget documents. Although a new president has since taken office and the campus is currently undergoing fiscal retrenchment, the program is well regarded and perceived to be solid. Many deans and department chairs promote the program when they recruit women faculty and encourage them to participate after they arrive.

The primary goal of most mentors is to help junior women deal with their individual situations as positively as possible. With the support and guidance of a savvy mentor, most junior women can manage the barriers and roadblocks associated with an academic career. There are times, however, when more is needed. Individual mentors have intervened in departmental matters on behalf of junior women. They have served as advocates, mediators, and sponsors. These activities suggest that the program is not merely serving the status quo but rather challenging the traditional norms and culture of the university. The short-term goal is the success of individual women; the long-term goal is to create a culture that will value and enable the success of all qualified women.

It is evident from the program assessments that both mentors and mentees value their experience in the program highly. The relationships they develop with their individual mentor or mentee are perceived as most beneficial, but the contacts initiated through group meetings and formal information sessions are also seen as invaluable. As one mentor stated, "I would say that in my entire career, from the time I entered graduate school until now, it is the single most empowering program that I've been associated with." The fact that this program is of value to both junior *and* senior women indicates the potential for building a strong women's community within the university—a community that can counter the isolation felt by so many women.

## Conclusion

Some academic women have expressed fear that mentoring junior women will reinforce the notion that women "don't have what it takes to make it" or will be perceived as hand-holding. Certainly, if the academy were a more receptive and welcoming culture that held to its principles of open-mindedness, fairness, and merit without regard to gender (or any other irrelevant characteristics, for that matter), we would not have to mentor women faculty. But as it is, the data are clear. Women too often feel as if they are not welcome, and consequently they leave the academy. If we want to engage the talents and energies of our brightest new women recruits, we must attend to their experience.

The program at the University of Hawaii has been designed to include a combination of strategies to achieve success. Women faculty who experience immediate attention to their adjustment and professional growth are more likely to want to stay after they are hired. To be effective, a mentoring program must meet the needs of individual faculty women, but also be a part of a general support system. Successful programs need visibility, administrative support, and just enough structure to facilitate worthwhile activities and to motivate participants to spend valuable time with one another. Successful programs also need sufficient data to facilitate program planning and assessment, to justify their continuation, and to provide evidence that they can, even in the short run, accomplish the goals of developing and retaining qualified faculty women. And in the long run, we will achieve the critical mass of tenured women faculty that is needed to support an academic culture that is a caring and receptive scholarly community.

## Note:

1.   For a complete description of the original pilot program, see M. A. Wunsch and L. K. Johnsrud, "Breaking Barriers: Mentoring Junior Faculty Women for Professional Development and Retention," published in *To Improve the Academy*, 1991, *11*, 175–187.

## References

Aisenberg, N., and Harrington, M. *Women of Academe: Outsiders in the Sacred Grove.* Amherst: University of Massachusetts Press, 1988.

Boice, R. "New Faculty Experiences of Women and Minorities: Four Levels of Analysis and Two Campuses." Unpublished manuscript, Faculty Instructional Support Office, State University of New York at Stony Brook, 1992.

Bourguignon, E., Blanshan, S. A., Chiteji, L., MacLean, K. J., Meckling, S. J., Sagaria, M. A., Shuman, A. E., and Taris, M. T. *Junior Faculty Life at Ohio State: Insights on Gender and Race.* Study by the Affirmative Action Program and the University Senate Committee on Women and Minorities. Columbus: Ohio State University, 1987.

Eveslage, S., A., Stonewater, B., and Dingerson, M. "Faculty Perceptions of Their Career Helping Relationships." Paper presented at the annual meeting of the Association for the Study of Higher Education, Baltimore, Nov. 1987.

Finkelstein, M. *The American Academic Profession: A Synthesis of Social Scientific Inquiry Since World War II.* Columbus: Ohio State University Press, 1984.

Johnsrud, L. K., and Atwater, C. D. *Barriers to Retention and Tenure at UH-Manoa: Faculty Cohorts 1982–1988.* Technical report, University of Hawaii, Honolulu, 1991a.

Johnsrud, L. K., and Atwater, C. D. "Women Faculty Mentoring Program Assessment, 1990–91." In the *Report on the Educational Improvement Fund 1990–91,* Office of Faculty Development and Academic Support, University of Hawaii at Manoa, 1991b.

Johnsrud, L., K., and Wunsch, M. A. "Junior and Senior Faculty Women: Commonalities and Differences in Perceptions of Academic Life." *Psychological Reports,* 1991a, *69,* 879–886.

Johnsrud, L. K., and Wunsch, M. A. "Barriers to Success in Academic Life: Perceptions of Faculty Women in a Colleague Pairing Program." Paper presented at the annual meeting of the Association for the Study of Higher Education, Boston, Nov. 1991b.

Kaufman, D. R. "Associational Ties in Academe: Some Male and Female Differences." *Sex Roles,* 1978, *4,* 9–21.

Menges, R. J., and Exum, W. H. "Barriers to the Progress of Women and Minority Faculty." *Journal of Higher Education,* 1983, *54,* 123–143.

Olsen, D., Maple, S. A., and Stage, F. "Women and Minority Faculty Job Satisfaction: A Structural Model Examining the Effect of Professional Role Interests, Professional Satisfactions, and Institutional Fit." Paper presented at the annual meeting of the Association for the Study of Higher Education, Boston, Nov. 1991.

Rausch, D. K., Ortiz, B. P., Douthitt, R. A ., and Reed, L. L. "The Academic Revolving Door: Why Do Women Get Caught?" *CUPA Journal,* 1989, *4,* 1–16.
Yoder, J. D. "An Academic Woman as Token: A Case Study." *Journal of Social Issues,* 1985, *41,* 61–72.

LINDA K. JOHNSRUD *is associate professor in the Department of Educational Administration at the University of Hawaii, Manoa.*

*Three mentoring programs, two for teaching development and one
for research development, for new faculty at the University of
Georgia are described.*

# Mentoring New Faculty for Teaching and Research

*William K. Jackson, Ronald D. Simpson*

The early years of a faculty member's career set the stage for a lifetime of
accomplishment, or failure, as a citizen of the academy. During what Baldwin
(1990) has characterized as "the entry period," new faculty members learn
institutional policies and procedures and become familiar with the aspirations
and values of their departments. It is during this period that new faculty members also begin to develop, and balance, their commitments to the two major
dimensions of their professional lives: research and teaching. They search for
ways of becoming both effective teachers and productive scholars. Unfortu-
nately, they enter this critical period at the very time that the powerful mentoring relationships of their student years are either weakened or lost entirely.
Some, especially minorities and women, may never have experienced mentoring at all. Many of these new faculty members feel isolated and alone (Boice,
1992) in a challenging new environment, where they are faced with more
demands than ever before (Schuster, 1990).

Research universities present a number of special challenges for new faculty members. At many of these institutions, demands for teaching effectiveness are increasing, while traditional demands for research productivity remain
unabated. At the same time, reduced funding opportunities make it more difficult for younger faculty to establish new research programs. The size and
complexity of the research university can amplify the feelings of isolation and
loneliness experienced by many new faculty members, and the relative autonomy enjoyed by each academic unit at a large university can lead to great vari-
ation in the support provided to new people. Although these problems
exist to some extent at most institutions, there is probably no other type of

institution where effective mentoring of new faculty members is needed more than in the research university.

The University of Georgia (UGA), a Carnegie Classification Research I University, serves as the flagship of the thirty-four-institution University System of Georgia. It is a single-campus land grant and sea grant institution enrolling approximately 28,000 students and employing approximately 2,000 faculty members. Each year about seventy-five new assistant professors join the university.

At UGA, systematic efforts to provide mentoring opportunities for new faculty members began in 1984 when eight senior faculty members became mentors for the first group of eight Lilly Teaching Fellows. From that modest beginning, mentoring opportunities for teaching development have now been extended to all new faculty members; faculty members in the behavioral and social sciences have the additional opportunity for mentoring related to their research. Together, these mentoring programs now reach forty to fifty new faculty members each year. In some cases a junior faculty member has been able to participate in all three of these programs.

## Lilly Teaching Fellows Program

The success of the Lilly Teaching Fellows program has been well documented (Austin, 1990). Since 1987, the program has been fully funded by the university as an ongoing activity of the Office of Instructional Development (OID).

**Selecting Participants.** Each year nine assistant professors who have been at the university for less than four years are selected to participate in this year long program designed to enhance their development as teachers and members of the university community. These nine Lilly Fellows are selected from a pool of approximately thirty-five applicants by a committee that includes OID staff and representatives of the current Lilly Fellow group. Each fellow receives funding for an individual instructional improvement project. In addition, each fellow is provided with a mentor selected from among the senior faculty. Members of the fellows group meet regularly throughout the year.

The difficulties many new faculty members experience are illuminated during the process of mentor selection in the Lilly program. Based on their written application materials, about one-half of the applicants for the Lilly program are interviewed by the selection commitee. During these interviews candidates are asked if they have someone in mind who they might like to have serve as their Lilly mentor. Many of the candidates are unable to identify a potential mentor. Frequently these candidates express concern because they feel isolated from the rest of the university. They note that if selected for the program, they will ask for assistance in identifying a mentor from outside of their home department. In some cases, Lilly candidates believe that a mentoring relationship within their department will align them too closely with one of several departmental factions. In other cases, the candidate already receives extensive support from the faculty within the home department and has several potential mentors in mind. One of the messages that emerges clearly from this interview process is that there is tremendous unevenness in the level of mentoring and other support provided by individual academic units to their new faculty members. The mentoring available in the Lilly program is one mechanism for compensating for this unevenness.

After the Lilly Fellows are selected, a mentor is appointed for each fellow. About half of these mentors are from the fellows' home departments. Mentors for the other fellows are drawn from a campuswide pool of senior faculty members who are considered to be excellent role models for junior colleagues. Once the fellow–mentor pair is established only a minimum amount of structure is imposed on the relationship. The mentors are invited to attend several of the Lilly group meetings and they also participate with the fellows in a three-day, end-of-year retreat on one of Georgia's coastal islands. Through these group activities the fellows share their mentors with their cohorts and each fellow benefits from the seasoned perspectives of all of the mentors.

**Program Activities.** The individual relationships between each fellow and her or his mentor vary. Some of these relationships develop around the fellow's individual project. For his project, a fellow in the criminal justice program developed a number of cases for use in an introductory course. This fellow selected a mentor who was interested in using case-study methods in her criminal justice courses, and they worked together on the development of these courses. A fellow in the Department of Housing and Consumer Economics wanted to develop a course on low income housing for her project. She was matched with a mentor from the real estate program in the College of Business, and they worked together to develop her course. Some fellows' projects benefit from the computer expertise or other technical capabilities of the mentors. In other cases, the mentors are not involved in the fellows' projects at all.

Some fellow–mentor relationships focus on observations and discussions of each other's teaching. A fellow who is teaching a large class for the first time might request a mentor who has experience with large classes. A fellow assigned an important course in the major might select a mentor who has taught the course previously. Some mentors serve as counselors or guides on a wide range of institutional issues such as promotion and tenure. At least half of these relationships continue beyond the fellowship year; indeed, it is common to observe, on a single day, several former fellows and their mentors having lunch together at the university's faculty center.

**Evaluation.** The Lilly Fellows program represents the university's first attempt to provide mentoring to new faculty in a systematic way. Although this program is relatively small, its impact is cumulative. After nine years, approximately 10 percent of the university's faculty have participated either as a fellow or as a mentor. The Lilly Endowment included UGA in a recent study of successful Lilly Teaching Fellow programs (Austin, 1990), and the program was judged beneficial and worthy of continued university support during three internal reviews of OID programs by panels of university faculty members and administrators. These reviews included examination of program goals and activities and interviews with program participants. Collaborations between fellows and mentors have resulted in a number of textbooks, laboratory manuals, and other nationally distributed instructional materials. And the success of this program from the perspectives of both the fellows and the mentors created impetus to extend the benefits of this program to all new faculty and to also provide mentoring opportunities focusing on the research dimension of a new faculty member's development.

## Teaching Improvement Program

The Teaching Improvement Program (TIPs) was conceived by a Lilly Teaching Fellow to provide junior faculty with a senior faculty teaching mentor (Diehl and Simpson, 1989). Junior faculty with no prior full-time teaching experience are targeted as mentees. The typical assistant professor has served as a teaching assistant during his or her graduate studies, but such experience often does not involve full responsibility for designing and teaching classes. Furthermore, the assistant professor is often assigned courses that require extensive planning and new preparations. Also, the junior faculty member probably has not discovered which instructional techniques are most suited to his or her teaching style or the specific needs of students. For these reasons, assistant professors during their first years in rank are the most appropriate subjects for programs designed to offer suggestions on improving teaching effectiveness. During the first two years of TIPs the staff made a decision to restrict the program to junior faculty members with a primary responsibility for undergraduate instruction. This decision was a function both of the need to limit the size of the program and to meet the university's renewed commitment to undergraduate teaching. This program was designed not only for those believed to be having difficulty in the classroom, but for those who wished to become better teachers. The assumption of TIPs is that even the best instructors can benefit from feedback and evaluation by a colleague.

**Selecting TIPs Mentors.** Mentors selected for TIPs are senior faculty members who have reputations for being excellent teachers. A senior faculty member with a distinguished teaching record can serve as a role model for the mentee, who may fear that only research will provide the rewards of academic life. To select potential TIPs mentors, we first identified those who had won university teaching awards. Next, we gathered names from among those who had served on the university instructional advisory committee. These individuals were recognized as having a strong commitment to excellence in teaching and a willingness to devote time and effort to that cause. Finally, we looked to those who had already served as mentors in the Lilly Fellows program. These individuals already had experience in working with junior faculty on teaching-related issues. From this list, the director of the OID sent letters to potential mentors, inviting each to consider serving as a mentor in the program. Included in this solicitation was a description of the program and the duties of a mentor.

Each fall at the university's colloquium for new faculty all new assistant professors receive information about the TIPs program. Typically twenty to thirty each year indicate interest and apply. Participants are spread across the three quarters of the academic calendar and are matched with suitable mentors. Primarily, mentors are chosen on the basis of the type of classes they teach and the comparability of their courses with those taught by the mentees. Consideration is also given to the teaching techniques employed by both individuals. For example, if a mentor from veterinary medicine were matched with a broadcast journalism mentee it might be because both have worked with small classes in a professional program and made extensive use of audio-visual materials. Although the departments of mentor and mentee are often different, care is spent in matching subject matter areas that correspond in some logical way. For example, someone in physics would usually be paired with someone in another quantitative area. As another example of logical assignment, a mentor from political science, who was an amateur musicologist, was paired with a mentee from the music school.

**Program Activities.** TIPs is designed for the mentor and mentee to meet two or three times over the course of a quarter. The first meeting, arranged by the TIPs staff, is a session to introduce the mentor and mentee. The next key meeting occurs when the mentor visits a class taught by the mentee. The mentor is instructed to observe the teaching performance and to be prepared to share observations with the mentee. The mentee is then invited to observe the teaching techniques of the mentor. The process is completed at a final meeting in which the mentor points out the strengths of the mentee's teaching and offers some suggestions on how classroom performance might be improved. Suggestions on teaching strategies, style, and other areas are appropriate points for discussion. Often the mentor and mentee agree to additional class visits and meetings. Sometimes this relationship goes on indefinitely.

Every academic unit gives some weight to teaching effectiveness in making salary, promotion, and tenure decisions. Any time a colleague visits another's class there is the risk that such observation could be used in the faculty evaluation process. To eliminate mentees' fears that information from TIPs would be used against them at a later time, a number of safeguards were established. First, the program is entirely voluntary. It does not force anyone into a situation in which he or she might be uncomfortable. Second, the mentor assigned to the junior faculty member must be from outside the home department, and in some cases even outside of the college, of the junior faculty member. This ensures that the junior faculty member is not made uncomfortable by a person who may make personnel decisions affecting him or her at a later time. Third, the mentor and the mentee must agree that the results of TIPs will remain entirely confidential. No written evaluation concerning the junior faculty member is rendered, and access to any consultation or information is restricted to the mentor and the mentee. With these safeguards, the purpose of improving instruction cannot be compromised by fears that information from the program will be used in matters of salary, promotion, and tenure.

**Impact of the Program.** Evaluation of TIPs has been positive. In response to a follow-up survey, 88 percent of the mentors and mentees responding strongly agreed with the statement: "Overall, TIPs is a valuable program." The other 12 percent merely agreed with the statement, indicating an endorsement of the program from all of its participants. Mentees reported receiving valuable suggestions from their mentors, including ideas for promoting class discussions, setting class expectations, and trying new teaching methods. Several mentors indicated that their mentees were already fine teachers and that the mentees actually helped give the mentors new insights about teaching. Therefore, the program appears to help both mentors and mentees with their classroom instruction.

Scheduling has been more than a trivial problem for this program. At the outset, scheduling conflicts force the staff each year to rematch mentees. More significantly, busy schedules for both the mentor and mentee cause delays in the process. In addition, leaving the responsibility of subsequent scheduling to the participants sometimes precipitates delays between meetings; occasionally, some prodding is necessary to get them back on track. Keeping the momentum going and achieving closure in a timely fashion is another challenge. While TIPs mentors have schedules much busier than the average faculty member, it seems that those identified as good teachers and willing to serve in the program are also in heavy demand for departmental and university committees. This is an unavoidable consequence of getting the best people to act as mentors.

## Institute for Behavioral Research Mentoring Program

The Institute for Behavioral Research (IBR) is an interdisciplinary unit of the office of the vice-president for research at UGA. In 1990, using the Lilly program as a model, the IBR established a mentoring program to facilitate the development of the research expertise of young faculty members.

**Selecting Participants.** Each year five faculty members are selected to participate in this program. Candidates are nominated by their department heads and screened by a panel of senior faculty members from the IBR. Although any faculty member is eligible to apply, the emphasis of the program is on assisting new faculty members in the development of successful strategies for obtaining extramural funding for their research. Each participant is paired for twelve months with a senior faculty member who serves as a mentor. As with the Lilly program, only about one half of the mentors are from the same department as their mentees.

**Program Activities.** During the yearlong mentoring period, the mentor assists the mentee with his or her research, and advises the mentee on the preparation of a proposal for extramural funding. Each mentee also receives a grant of $3,000 to facilitate his or her research and each mentor receives a $500 discretionary grant to partially compensate her or him for the time she or he invests in the program. This mentoring program also includes a number of group activities. Seminars are scheduled on topics related to research and extramural funding in the social and behavioral sciences, and an end-of-year retreat is held at which the mentees' projects are presented and the program is evaluated.

**Evaluation.** Although the IBR Mentoring program is still quite new, the impact of this program is already evident (Institute for Behavioral Research, 1992). During the first three years, fifteen mentees participated in this program. All of these individuals submitted grant applications and eleven obtained external funding for their research. This program has already proven to be successful in the development of the grant-seeking skills of new faculty members in the social and behavioral sciences and it continues to serve as the major faculty development activity of the IBR. From the beginning, funding for this mentoring program has been provided by the institution.

## Conclusions

What have we learned?

- The success of these three programs is a clear indication that there is a need for formal mentoring programs for faculty who are in the entry stage of their careers.
- There will always be a pool of senior faculty members who are both capable and willing to serve as mentors for their junior colleagues.
- Mentoring across departmental boundaries is feasible, and in some cases necessary.
- Providing mentoring options outside of the mentee's department requires the mentoring program to be administered above the departmental level.
- The important human dimension—one person helping another—is the key to success.

## References

Austin, A. E. *To Leave an Indelible Mark: Encouraging Good Teaching Through Faculty Development.* Nashville, Tenn.: Vanderbilt University, 1990.
Baldwin, R. G. "Faculty Career Stages and Implications for Professional Development." In J. H. Schuster, D. W. Wheeler, and Associates, *Enhancing Faculty Careers: Strategies for Development and Renewal.* San Francisco: Jossey-Bass, 1990.
Boice, R. *The New Faculty Member: Supporting and Fostering Professional Development.* San Francisco: Jossey-Bass, 1992.

Diehl, P. F., and Simpson, R. D. "Investing in Junior Faculty: The Teaching Improvement Program (TIPs)." *Innovative Higher Education,* 1989, *13* (2), 147–157.

Institute for Behavioral Research. *Annual Report: 1991–1992.* Athens: Institute for Behavioral Research, University of Georgia, 1992.

Schuster, J. F. "The Need for Fresh Approaches to Faculty Renewal." In J. H. Schuster, D. W. Wheeler, and Associates, *Enhancing Faculty Careers: Strategies for Development and Renewal.* San Francisco: Jossey-Bass, 1990.

WILLIAM K. JACKSON *is associate director of the Office of Instructional Development at the University of Georgia.*

RONALD D. SIMPSON *is professor of science education and higher education and director of the Office of Instructional Development at the University of Georgia.*

*A peer mentoring process for part-time faculty not only ensures
their teaching skill development, but breaks down colleague
isolation and contributes to their institutional commitment.*

# Forging the Ties That Bind:
# Peer Mentoring Part-Time Faculty

*Barbara J. Millis*

In a recent book Boice (1992) paints a bleak picture of the academic landscape
faced by new faculty members. Isolated and uncertain, they receive little support during their first few years in traditional academia. If these carefully
selected, long-term faculty members receive so little support, the fate of thou-
sands of part-time faculty members must be far worse. Despite predictions
made over fifteen years ago that the use of part-time faculty would decline in
the 1980s (Leslie, 1978, cited in Shulman, 1979), part-timers are now in fact
a permanent part of the academic work force and teach substantial parts of the
undergraduate curriculum (Gappa, 1993). In fact, Masters (1992) notes that
Department of Education statistics indicate that their ranks grew 18 percent
from 1983 to 1989, to 299,794.

Too often, despite their numbers, part-time faculty—defined as less-than-
full-time, teaching-oriented faculty, in non-tenure-track positions—are treated
as second-class, marginal employees. Despite strong evidence that part-time
faculty members bring to institutions strong academic credentials often aug-
mented by "real-world" experience, plus enthusiasm and energetic approaches
to teaching (Gappa and Leslie, 1993), they often receive neither the respect
nor the support their contributions deserve. In some cases, they meet with out-
right hostility from full-time faculty members who believe as does Pratt (cited
in Mangan, 1991, p. 9) that the employment of part-timers is an indirect
assault on the tenure system. Isolation from colleagues and the academic community are often the unfortunate result of what Stone (1993) calls the "Maytag syndrome." In some institutions, however, such as the University of
Maryland University College (UMUC), the part-time faculty are strongly supported and highly integrated into the university's mission.

NEW DIRECTIONS FOR TEACHING AND LEARNING, no. 57, Spring 1994  © Jossey-Bass Publishers

## University of Maryland University College Setting

One of the eleven campuses of the University of Maryland System, UMUC prides itself on its teaching mission and its responsiveness to adult learners. Because 700–800 undergraduate courses a semester, offered throughout the state of Maryland including military installations, are taught solely by part-time lecturers (called interchangeably "adjunct" lecturers), UMUC feels a strong ethical responsibility to see that these key individuals receive the support and the recognition they warrant. These lecturers tend to be intrinsically motivated, highly committed adjuncts who bring both academic and professional credentials to the classroom. They care about teaching, an avocation for them, and they welcome support. Like the adult students they serve, they need and deserve respect, validation, and opportunities for growth.

UMUC students tend to be intrinsically motivated, self-directed learners, who, in this era of educational accountability, are also both discerning and demanding. UMUC is serious about its commitment to serving a diverse student population: 51 percent of the students are female, 29 percent are minorities. Because of a flexible admissions policy and a welcoming climate, many students arrive underprepared, disadvantaged, or simply far removed in time from former academic endeavors.

UMUC recognizes that new student populations require new responses in the classroom. In particular, faculty members must be helped to appreciate and capitalize on the experiences that adults from a variety of backgrounds bring to the classroom. Likewise, they must know how to reach a broad range of students with the aid of more diverse teaching approaches. Adams (1992), for example, emphasizes "the flexibility of a college instructor's teaching repertoire, and his or her readiness to draw on a range of teaching styles for a variety of ends" (p. 15). Gaff (1992) suggests that "business-as-usual" pedagogical approaches such as relying exclusively on lecturing, requiring rote memorization, or using only multiple choice tests, will block the learning of too many students. To fulfill UMUC's teaching mission and meet the needs of its diverse student population, lecturers, despite their part-time status, must be unusually skilled. Thus, UMUC cannot—and does not—pay lip service to its teaching mission. Lecturers must be fully equipped with a broad range of teaching strategies to motivate and facilitate student learning. They must also feel committed to the institution and to its teaching mission. A strong, viable faculty development program helps UMUC achieve these goals.

## Overview of Peer Mentoring at University of Maryland University College

UMUC supports a comprehensive, wide-ranging, well-administered faculty development program, designed in all respects, including meetings scheduled for evening and weekend hours, for adjunct lecturers. Activities include new faculty orientations, general and discipline-specific faculty meetings, a workshop series, faculty newsletters, a teaching portfolio initiative, student course evaluations, excellence in teaching awards, and teaching-related travel grants. The most significant component of this program is a two-term mentoring program—one of the few in the country designed for part-time faculty—that rests on the one-on-one consultations occurring in conjunction with peer visits.[1]

Emphasizing collegiality and the value of positive change, the Peer Mentor Program was initiated in 1985 and expanded in 1990—with support from the Fund for the Improvement of Postsecondary Education (FIPSE)—to include a follow-up visit. The Office of Faculty Development schedules over seventy visits a semester. The two primary target groups are adjunct faculty new to UMUC (about sixty each semester) and all faculty (over seventy a year) nominated for the Excellence in Teaching Award.

Adjunct faculty new to UMUC are introduced to the mentoring program during their initial application interviews. They are assured that they will receive ongoing support: the support will include a visit by a teaching colleague in the same or a related discipline. Discipline matches are always made in the case of highly specialized, upper-level courses. In other instances, a discipline match is desirable, but not necessary, given the fact that experienced visitors participate in intensive, ongoing three-hour training workshops. Furthermore, Weimer (1988) and others have emphasized that trained observers are able to report accurately on teaching processes regardless of their discipline orientation. In fact, because lecturers in the same discipline may enter a classroom convinced that their approach to teaching a given topic is the best one, observers from outside disciplines may give more objective feedback about teaching effectiveness.

The Peer Mentoring Program has always received strong support from the highest levels of the administration, beginning with the president. The well-funded program is administered by the assistant dean for faculty development. Its day-to-day functions are carried out by a half-time administrative coordinator. Mentors are paid a stipend of $50.00 for an initial visit/consultation and $35.00 for a follow-up visit. The program is also well supported by administrative computing. A specially designed software program facilitates matching the mentors to the mentees and generating the correspondence associated with the peer visits.

Besides strong administrative support for the Peer Mentoring Program and its integration within a comprehensive faculty development program, several key factors contribute to its success. The first of these is the emphasis on collegiality.

## Colleagues Helping Colleagues

The heart of the Peer Mentoring Program is a philosophy of professional collegiality: colleagues helping colleagues. Although classroom observations are the catalyst for faculty–faculty contacts, we emphasize that the visit itself is merely part of the consultation process, not an end in itself. The value of one-on-one consultation for improving teaching effectiveness has been well documented in the literature. Erickson and Erickson (1979), for instance, note: "Instructors who go through the teaching consultation procedure make qualitative changes in their teaching skill performance which are evident to students in subsequent courses. . . . The results also indicate that the improvements in their teaching skill performance are relatively long-lived" (p. 682).

Furthermore, faculty themselves feel positively toward instructional consultation with colleagues. Menges (1987) notes that "as far as faculty participants are concerned . . . findings are clear [about the effectiveness of colleagues as consultants]: participants report high satisfaction, more interaction with other faculty members, increased motivation, and renewed interest in teaching" (p. 91). A survey conducted by the Faculty Development Total Quality Management (TQM) Committee confirmed this finding for UMUC faculty. Of the seventy-three lecturers, which included both those who served as mentors and those who were mentees, who responded to the questionnaire, 83 percent "agreed" or "strongly agreed" that the program positively affects teaching behavior through improvement and reinforcement of effective teaching practices and that it provides opportunities for mutual learning experiences. This emphasis on "mutuality" or reciprocality is central to the program.

Gladstone (1987) defines a mentor as "someone who helps another person become what that person aspires to be" (p. 9) and suggests that the cycle of mentoring is completed when mentees become mentors themselves, as happens fairly often in UMUC's program. Many of those nominated for the Excellence in Teaching Award serve as peer mentors. Thus, despite the typical view of a mentor as a guide, particularly in the case of the award nominees the relationship is more reciprocal. In fact, we encourage this collegial, egalitarian approach. Because most faculty hired by UMUC are already experienced teachers (only 22.2 percent have never taught before, according to 162 respondents at the mandatory new faculty orientation sessions held each semester), the interactions between the mentor and the mentee assume a positive, often reciprocal tone. In fact, faculty active in the peer mentoring program consistently comment that the experience enhances their skills as teachers, and that they are certain that they learn as much from the interaction with the new faculty members, particularly through the classroom observation, as they learn from them. As Sands, Parson, and Duane (1991) point out, mentoring is a complex, dynamic, multidimensional process.

For example, in a recent issue of *Faculty Focus*, UMUC's teaching newsletter, Rajiv Kohli, a computer applications adjunct lecturer, described his experiences with the Peer Mentoring Program. A fellow adjunct who visited his "Survey of Artificial Intelligence Applications" course in 1989 invited him to meet several of his colleagues at Westinghouse who were working on projects related to Rajiv's interests in decision support systems and artificial intelligence applications. As a result of their subsequent collaboration, Rajiv became involved with netting a $150,000 grant that enabled him to publish several research papers and to continue joint efforts with Westinghouse engineers. After his nomination for UMUC's Excellence in Teaching Award, Rajiv became a peer mentor himself.

The Peer Mentoring Program at UMUC thus deliberately downplays the more traditional model of a mentor as a seasoned, experienced individual guiding and advising a dependent subordinate. Several adjunct faculty reported that their visits enabled them to identify qualified substitutes who could cover their classes during occasional business-related absences. One mentor even located a neighborhood babysitter, the daughter of her mentee!

Besides the emphasis on reciprocal collegiality, the Peer Mentoring Program is successful because of its professional, systematic administration.

## Peer Mentor Process

To match mentors with mentees, the coordinator uses peer visit preference forms returned by visitors before each term and the course information on the computerized faculty data base. The scheduling software enables him to identify appropriate mentors (usually from the same discipline as the mentee) who are available on the necessary days to visit evening and weekend classes in far-flung locations throughout the state of Maryland. (One dedicated peer mentor recently accompanied a historian nominated for the Excellence in Teaching Award on an all-day class field trip to Gettysburg!) He also makes certain that the mentors are scheduled for follow-up visits with their mentees.

The scheduling letter suggests a date for the classroom observation. The instructional consultation process between mentors and mentees is clearly explained in the scheduling letter and in the peer visit packet sent to both the mentor and the mentee. The packet contains (1) an overview of the program, including a peer mentor process flow chart and visit guidelines; (2) resources for the mentee, including multiple self-assessment instruments, advice about receiving feedback and using it constructively to implement changes, and areas of possible feedback; and (3) resources for the mentor, including characteristics of constructive feedback; guidelines for preparing the classroom visit form, which focuses the observation; and examples of concrete feedback. To emphasize collegiality, enclosed with the scheduling letter sent by the Office of Faculty Development is a one-page information sheet prepared by the mentee. It gives her/his academic background, but also expresses views concerning personal teaching philosophies that may spark substantive discussions. Mentees, in turn, send to their mentors they syllabus and any other relevant course materials.

Then, prior to the visit, when the mentor contacts the new part-time lecturer or the Excellence in Teaching Award nominee, they can discuss the visit within the broad context of the course objectives; the previous class meetings and assignments; the classroom climate, including student motivation and their preparation; and the physical setting. They can also look at the immediate context of the class the mentor will visit: What are the objectives for that particular evening? How do they relate to the broader course goals? What activities will occur and why does the lecturer feel they will promote the overall course objectives? How comfortable is the lecturer with the class activities: is risk taking involved or is this "business as usual" for the lecturer and the students?

When the mentors visit classes, the guidelines in the peer visit packet suggest that they should be introduced to students, thus enlarging the sphere of collegiality. In fact, lecturers are encouraged to announce the nature and purpose of the mentor visit a week ahead of time, so that students can appreciate UMUC's investment in teaching excellence, but more importantly, so that they won't "clam up" at the sight of a stranger in the classroom. Too often, classroom observations have been conducted as though the visitor were sitting in the back row in a trench coach with a concealed notepad to help get the "lowdown" on a professor's incompetence.

Following the visit, which typically lasts about an hour and fifteen minutes, the visitors share their observations in a supportive, constructive manner, recognizing, as Robert Wilson (1986) notes, that "the more behavioral, specific, or concrete a suggestion is, the more likely it is that it will affect students' perceptions of his or her teaching" (p. 206). The visitor forwards the completed classroom visit form to the Office of Faculty Development where the coordinator and the assistant dean of faculty development summarize the comments and offer, when appropriate, specific advice, including changes in classroom activities or follow-up instructional improvement opportunities, such as workshops. The exchanges, even when problems surface, are always positive and collegial; usually the letters provide a "pat on the back," which can be included with other professional credentials. In all aspects of the Peer Mentoring Program, UMUC strives for quality and professionalism, both in the process and in the people.

## Peer Mentors

The selection and training of peer mentors is undertaken with care. Each summer the assistant dean of faculty development compiles a list of potential mentors composed of nominees for the Excellence in Teaching Award and those adjunct lecturers who have scored 4.75 or above on their student evaluations, thus receiving a letter of commendation from the dean. Thus, only those who are known and respected for their teaching expertise are considered. A guiding credo might be Alexander's Pope's admonition: "Let such teach others who themselves excel." But teaching expertise is only a part of the whole. Daloz (1990) paints a rich portrait of Virgil as an ideal mentor: someone who engenders trust, provides support, issues challenges, and offers vision. UMUC expects a great deal from mentors beyond just knowing course content. Mentors must be able to communicate clearly and warmly all the broad parameters of teaching, including the most effective ways to meet the needs of diverse adult students. Before inviting these experienced adjuncts to serve as peer mentors, the coordinator asks the assistant deans and program managers who staff the courses, and who thus know the faculty best, to screen the list of candidates. Only those with strong interpersonal skills are invited to join the program. We agree with Centra (1979) that "trained observers make sounder judgments than untrained observers" (p. 76). Thus, three-hour training sessions are conducted each fall. Both new mentors and experienced ones are invited to explore the complexities of conducting peer observations and providing constructive feedback. We have used a number of approaches, including small-group exercises, role plays, and case studies. We also discuss directly through a series of carefully delineated steps (Millis, 1992) how the mentor program works in its entirety. During training we provide mentors with positive examples of peer observation reviews that are recorded on the peer visit form, and an example of focused narrative, which allows flexible, concrete feedback. The quality of the mentors has been exceptional. Part-time faculty who are successful in many fields (for example, a brigadier general, judges, a high-ranking American Association for Higher Education professional), willingly devote hours of their lives to what Russell Edgerton (1988) characterizes as "collegial dialogues" in a "culture in which peer review of teaching is as common as peer review of research" (p. 8).

We feel that UMUC's Peer Mentoring Program has been an unqualified success. It has (1) provided a systematic, cost-effective, positive way to improve faculty effectiveness and to ensure "quality control" and accountability; (2) fostered a sense of faculty collegiality and a sense of pride in UMUC's teaching mission, thus improving retention and commitment; and (3) demonstrated to students and faculty the importance University College places on excellence in the classroom. Perhaps most significant is the sense of community and cooperation built by "colleagues helping colleagues." As Palmer (1987) notes, "Knowing and learning are communal acts. They require a continual cycle of discussion, disagreement, and consensus over what has been and what it all means" (p. 24).

## Note

1.    In UMUC's literature, this program is referred to as a Peer Visit Program. Because of the program's relevance to this publication and because of the fluid definition of "mentoring," reference throughout this chapter will be to "peer mentoring."

# References

Adams, M. "Cultural Inclusion in the American College Classroom." In N.V.N. Chism and L. L. Border (eds.), *Teaching for Diversity.* New Directions for Teaching and Learning, no. 49. San Francisco: Jossey-Bass, 1992.

Boice, R. *The New Faculty Member: Supporting and Fostering Professional Development.* San Francisco: Jossey-Bass, 1992.

Centra, J. A. *Assessing Teaching, Research, and Service for Personnel Decisions and Improvement. Determining Faculty Effectiveness:* San Francisco: Jossey-Bass, 1979.

Daloz, L. A. *Effective Teaching and Mentoring: Realizing the Transformational Power of Adult Learning Experiences.* San Francisco: Jossey-Bass, 1990.

Edgerton, R. "All Roads Lead to Teaching." *AAHE Bulletin,* 1988, *40* (8), 3–9.

Erickson, G. R., and Erickson, B. L. "Improving College Teaching: An Evaluation of a Teaching Consultation Procedure." *Journal of Higher Education,* 1979, *50,* 670–683.

Gaff, J. G. "Beyond Politics: The Educational Issues Inherent in Multicultural Education." *Change,* Jan.–Feb. 1992, pp. 31–35.

Gappa, J. M. "Integrating the Invisible Faculty: Strengthening Academic Programs with Part-Timers." Presentation at the American Association for Higher Education's National Conference on Higher Education, Washington, D.C., Mar. 1993.

Gappa, J. M., and Leslie, D. W. *The Invisible Faculty: Improving the Status of Part-Timers in Higher Education.* San Francisco: Jossey-Bass, 1993.

Gladstone, M. S. *Mentoring as an Educational Strategy in a Rapidly Changing Society.* Quebec, Canada: John Abbott College Research and Development Secretariat, 1987.

Mangan, K. S. "Many Colleges Fill Vacancies with Part-Time Professors, Citing Economy and Uncertainty About Enrollments." *Chronicle of Higher Education,* Aug. 7, 1991, pp. A9–A10.

Masters, B. A. "Part-Time Profs: New Campus Class." *Washington Post,* Oct. 21, 1992, pp. A1, A7.

Menges, R. J. "Colleagues as Catalysts for Change in Teaching." *To Improve the Academy,* 1987, *6,* 83–93.

Millis, B. J. "Conducting Effective Peer Classroom Observations." *To Improve the Academy,* 1992, *11,* 189–206.

Palmer, P. J. "Community, Conflict, and Ways of Knowing: Ways to Deepen Our Educational Agenda." *Change,* 1987, *19,* (5), 20–25.

Sands, R. G., Parson, L. A., and Duane, J. "Faculty Mentoring Faculty in a Public University." *Journal of Higher Education,* 1991, *62* (2), 175–193.

Shulman, C. H. *Old Expectations, New Realities: The Academic Profession Revisited.* AAHE-ERIC/Higher Education Research Report, no. 2. Washington, D.C.: American Association for Higher Education, 1979.

Stone, T. E. "Adjunct Lecturers and the Maytag Syndrome." *Teaching and Learning News,* 1993, *2* (3), 2.

Weimer, M. G. Higher Education: Faculty Evaluation, Faculty Development. Seminar taught at the University of Maryland University College Center of Adult Education.

Wilson, R. C. "Improving Faculty Teaching: Effective Use of Student Evaluations and Consultations." *Journal of Higher Education,* 1986, *57* (2), 196–209.

*BARBARA J. MILLIS is assistant dean for faculty development, University College, University of Maryland, College Park, Md.*

*A discipline-specific mentoring program in a department will encourage the new colleague to grow and develop within that disciplinary context. This, in turn, is essential for progress toward and ultimate attainment of tenure and promotion. The successful colleague retained by the institution is a manifestation of wise stewardship of institutional resources and of service to ourselves as persons.*

# Mentoring Faculty at the Departmental Level

*Kay U. Herr*

Mentoring in the context of the academic department, like mentoring in any other situation, is nothing new. It has been occurring since colleges and universities began organizing as complex structures. As the organizational units of higher education have become ever more complex and as we have become more aware of the need to value and to nurture our human resources, however, it is timely to consider the issues involved in mentoring faculty at the departmental level in comparison to cross-disciplinary or institutionally based mentoring. It is becoming even more critical to consider enhancing mentoring for new faculty in light of the demographic forecasts for the American professoriate.

Does mentoring work best at the department level? Does cross-discipline mentoring work better? Same-sex mentoring? Same-race mentoring? The literature, whether research studies or anecdotal reports, provides us with no clear-cut answers to these questions. Indeed, there is a lack of reports or studies focusing solely on departmentally based mentoring programs. Perhaps we should not expect clear and definitive answers for what seems to be a kind of natural human interaction. A recent, well-designed study of cross-discipline mentoring by Boice (1990) comes to the conclusion that "success in mentoring depends on what mentors do, not on who mentors are" (p. 154). We do know, however, that mentoring occurs at the departmental level. And we know that an effective mentoring relationship will benefit individuals involved and the institution. We can describe what constitutes mentoring at the

Bibliographical assistance was provided by Nancy L. Reed, a Ph.D. candidate in the Staff Development Program at Colorado State University and a student intern in the Office of Instructional Services.

departmental level, identify principles to guide departmental mentoring, and highlight some sample approaches.

The department, as it is understood within the structure of institutions of higher education, is the structural unit in what is commonly a hierarchical structure moving from department to school or college, and central institutional structures. It is the disciplinary division most common in American higher education. In smaller institutions and in community colleges the smallest structural unit may be a division; that term generally connotes a grouping of allied disciplines such as natural sciences or humanities. However, the terms *division, school, center,* or *institute* are also used in some institutions to describe the structural unit for one discipline, which is the focus of this chapter. For the sake of simplicity, here the word *department* will be used to describe this discipline-specific unit—a structure to be found in all of academe. While some disciplines may have clearly delineated subcategories, these smaller units are not ordinarily structural or organizational units in themselves. However, they may be the unit through which a departmental-based mentoring program is implemented.

The department is therefore the smallest management unit of an institution, and the persons in the department will be most closely bound by their common academic interests and experiences. Just as a university or college will have an organizational culture, so too will a department have a subculture, which will be a blend of the traditions of the discipline, the institutional culture, and the collective culture as built and contributed to by the persons within that department—both past and present.

What happens at the departmental level, both formally and informally, has a strong impact on the performance of each individual faculty member. For example, a dynamic and creative chairperson can enliven a department and lead it in new directions. A conservative and powerful departmental committee structure can, even though it may be unintentional, squelch, or certainly make more difficult, the efforts of a new and junior faculty member to introduce change or innovation. If departments do not cooperate in institutional efforts to change, the desired change is unlikely to be effected to any significant degree. In short, the department is a key management structure, and the department chairperson is a key management figure. It is at this level that the performance and growth of the new faculty member can best be encouraged and monitored.

## Aspects of Departmental Mentoring

Mentoring at the departmental level can mean several different things. It might mean the assignment of one person from within the department to serve as a mentor for the new faculty member. It might mean that two or more mentors will split certain responsibilities for a mentee. It could also mean that a search or hiring committee as a whole will serve as "mentor" to new faculty. The mentor within the department could also join with another mentor from outside the department. Mentoring could also include a variety of developmental activities designed to assist the new faculty member, perhaps organized and presented by a faculty development unit.

A departmental mentoring program could, and should, include provision for introduction to the following topics, among others:

- Assistance with teaching matters, with regard to the common elements of good pedagogical practices as well as elements related to discipline-specific pedagogy
- Introduction to professional organizations and professional networking
- Assistance with research activities, which might include involvement in joint efforts, grant writing, and introductions to key persons on campus
- The subculture of the department, the college or administrative level above the department, and the institution
- The workings, including committee structures, of the organizational units within the institution
- Introduction to issues of academic governance
- Socialization to the community of the institution and the community at large.

The first four of the above topics—discipline-specific pedagogical matters, professional organizations and context, research assistance, and introduction to the subculture of the department—are best covered at the departmental level. Indeed, they could not be addressed by a mentor from elsewhere. A system of cross-discipline or institutional mentoring can supplement the departmental focus, but the acculturation of the individual will be less than complete if the departmentally based activities are lacking, or spotty at best.

There can also, however, be a disadvantage to mentoring solely from within a department, particularly within a department at an institution with high research expectations. This disadvantage arises from the limited pool of potential mentors and from the differences in the expectations of new faculty of today as compared to the generation of older, senior faculty members and from differences in the changing expectations of society for higher education. New faculty may have more awareness and flexibility in the balance between teaching and research and more understanding of the increasing importance of educational technologies. For such reasons, one experiment with and study of mentoring (Boice and Turner, 1989) employed relatively junior—and one assumes tenured—faculty and cross-discipline pairings: "Our reasons for pairing mentors and mentees across traditional boundaries went beyond a curiosity about practicality. On a campus where many senior faculty might not have been appropriate mentors for new faculty faced with pressures to excel at both teaching and research, we turned to relatively junior faculty as an additional source of mentors. And on a campus where proportionately more new faculty were women and minorities, we looked beyond their immediate departments for mentoring sources" (p. 117).

## Principles of Mentoring at Departmental Level

As suggested above, our educational systems have become far more complex than they used to be, and, in many instances we now have to plan, organize, and promote what previously might have happened on a simpler level as a manifestation of natural human interaction. We can indeed plan, organize, and promote mentoring so that it happens in a systematic way. The first principle of department—or even institutional—mentoring is that it be *purposeful and planned* in recognition of the complexity of our systems and the often hectic nature of our professional academic life. If we leave mentoring to chance, it may or may not occur, and, even if it does occur it might not be as effective as we would hope. The stimulus to introduce purposeful and planned mentoring might come from a faculty committee or the department chairperson if such a program has not been mandated by the institution.

A departmental-based mentoring program must also be *reflective of the structure and culture of the unit and the institution.* For example, a large department with subdivisions and a tight organizational approach is unlikely to succeed with promotion of a departmental mentoring program if it comes forth simply as a suggestion from the chairperson or a committee. Rather, it would need to be more formalized. In contrast, a small department might not require a similar kind of organizational rigor to promote mentoring. A small institution with fewer written rules and policies than a larger, more complex institution might succeed in promoting departmental mentoring simply by suggestion and encouragement from central administrative officers, while the large institution might need written policy. If there is a clash between the impetus for a mentoring program and the structure and subculture of the institution, the mentoring program is less likely to be accepted and to succeed.

A third principle is the *recognition of individual differences.* Clearly, some new colleagues would do well with a strong and assertive mentoring relationship while others need and want only occasional gentle guidance. One senior faculty member may be more inclined to mentor with a strong hand while another may wait to be asked or invited to assist the mentee. In some instances, one mentor may offer the guidance necessary in all areas of importance—teaching, research, and service—while in another case the new faculty member might best be served by several mentors. A newly tenured faculty member at Colorado State University commented recently in a workshop for untenured faculty, "The whole department was my mentor—I used everyone for different reasons."

*Responsiveness to the needs and interests* of the new faculty member, as well as those of the mentor, is another principle that should characterize the departmental mentoring program. This principle is related to the principle calling for recognition of individual differences. If, for example, a faculty member comes to the institution with a particular area of research activity, the departmental mentor should obviously have an interest and a degree of expertise in that area. If an individual joins the department with an appointment as an extension specialist, a mentor working on basic research might not be the best choice. The new faculty member bubbling over with creative teaching ideas would be well paired with a similarly enthusiastic senior faculty member.

I would be remiss in not mentioning diversity issues in relationship to a mentoring program or system. Indeed, these should be taken into consideration. These issues are, however, a part of being responsive to individual differences, needs, and interests which should be the foremost factor in the pairing of mentor and mentee. There is no convincing evidence that same-gender, same-race, or same-ethnicity mentorship is any more likely to be successful than a relationship formed without such commonality. Boice and Turner (1989) concluded in their study of mentoring for new faculty with both discipline-specific and cross-disciplinary pairs as follows: "Perhaps the most useful finding was that pairings worked equally well within or across traditional boundaries of mentoring new faculty. That is, mentors evidenced the same high level of effectiveness whether they were senior or relatively junior, same or opposite sex of the mentee, same or different discipline as the mentee, or same or different ethnicity as the mentee" (p. 126). Also, in some instances it may not be possible to arrange a racially or ethnically common mentor–mentee relationship, and it is still the case in too many departments that a gender pairing for women is impossible. Another study (Luna and Cullen, 1992) focusing on the mentoring of women and minorities in higher education, offers the following conclusion: "With the complexity of conceptual frameworks within the mentoring process, what is clear is that mentoring means different things for different people. Therefore, customized professional mentoring programs are often more suitable and beneficial to women and minorities" (p. 135). Thus, the person or persons assigning mentors and mentees must make a judgment call. If it is felt that the mentor relationship would benefit by a gender, racial, or ethnic match and if this is not possible at the departmental level, than such a pairing might be accomplished by arranging a cross-disciplinary connection to complement a mentorship within the department.

The foremost principle is that of *flexibility*. If a mentoring program is flexible, it will adjust to the structure and subculture of the unit, it will function in recognition of individual differences, and it will be responsive to the needs and interests of the individuals involved. Clearly, any system must have a degree of flexibility, or it will be nonfunctional and atrophied. A flexible system will also allow for mid-course correction in recognition of the fact that not every purposefully and thoughtfully established mentor relationship—despite our best efforts and intentions—will work out perfectly. Bernice Sandler (1933) of the Center for Women Policy Studies recently identified potential pitfalls in the mentoring relationship such as the difficulty a mentor may have in letting go of the relationship or the possibility of exploitation of the mentee.

## Sample Approaches

"Soft-Sell" Approach. At Colorado State University a survey of new faculty from the previous school year was conducted in 1987 to assess perceptions about the mentoring they had received. At that time there had been no formal institutional encouragement to planned mentoring. The results of the survey were quite positive and encouraging, with 81 percent of respondents indicating one specific person had been particularly helpful to them in their first year. Specific questions were asked about elements of academic mentoring such as level of conversations about teaching and professional development opportunities, research grant information, offers to introduce the mentee to people, information about committees, and a variety of other topics. In the following spring a letter was sent to departments from the vice-president for academic affairs to encourage the establishment of mentoring at the department level. The letter noted, "It is a demographic fact that we are facing future potential shortages in the professoriate, and recruitment and retention of new faculty members are likely to become more significant issues in the next few years than they now are. Purposeful and planned mentoring also recognizes our collegial responsibility to help new associates with resettlement and adjustment to our institution and with assistance in their career development" (A. J. Linck, Colorado State University, memorandum, February 10, 1988). No prescription was provided, and no mandate was given. As of 1990, twenty-one of fifty-seven departments indicated that they had a "formalized mentoring program," and that number has continued to grow as a voluntary response. If funds allocated to diversity goals have been used in completing the new hire, however, it is an institutional requirement that a formal mentoring plan for the new faculty member be approved by the Office of the Provost/Academic Vice-President and be on file.

As a consequence of institutional encouragement rather than institutional mandate, different ways of introducing mentoring have arisen. These different ways reflect the specific situations of departments, their subculture, organizational structures, and overall organizational culture. An example of a formalized departmental mentoring policy is found in the Department of Food Science and Nutrition (no date) departmental code:

> It is the policy to provide all untenured and/or new faculty members with one or more peer mentor(s). The role of the mentor is to provide insight into the working of the University, college, and department; including its

history, expectations and general knowledge about the institution. This knowledge can aid the individual in the successful and efficient performance of his or her research, teaching, and outreach duties, and also enhance their potential to obtain tenure and/or rank advancement. It is recognized that individuals will wish to identify their mentor(s); however, to initiate the mentoring process, the department head will assign mentors to the new faculty member at the time the person arrives on campus. In most instances, the mentors will have been members of the Search Committee. After a period of 6–12 months, the new faculty member is encouraged to identify individuals who will better fill his or her mentoring needs and inform the department head of the change(s). All untenured faculty and/or instructors, assistant and associate professors are encouraged to have mentors. [pp. 8–9]

The Department of Civil Engineering, a very large department, took a different approach and created an assistant professors forum under the guidance of one senior faculty member and in combination with an individualized mentor pairing. The group met regularly for both formal and informal presentations and assisted in setting its own agenda. After two years there was consensus that its goals had been accomplished, and meetings ceased. An atmosphere favorable to more informal mentoring activities had been established through this forum.

Stephen D. Roper, a former chairperson of the Department of Anatomy and Neurobiology at Colorado State, prepared a detailed and thoughtful explanation of a "Mentoring System," which first appeared in the *Chairperson's Manual,* a publication prepared in 1989 by the faculty development unit and since then routinely distributed to new chairpersons at Colorado State. Professor Roper articulated the following components of this system, which calls for far more than simply assigning a mentor. It is a system that begins before the new colleague has even arrived on campus. He explains as follows:

- Provide the newly hired faculty member a clear explanation of what is expected over the next few years.
- Recognize that the transition from Ph.D. graduate or postdoctoral fellow to a new faculty member is a major change.
- Protect the newly hired faculty member from an overburdensome teaching/service load in the first year.
- Provide appropriate resources as start-up funds.
- Assure the availability of assistance in writing grants and preparing publications.
- Monitor the new faculty member's interaction with other faculty.
- Point out how a faculty member can obtain national visibility.
- Explain how and when tenure evaluation will be made.

- Recognize that everyone, but especially a new faculty member, needs to feel wanted and needed!
- Meet with the new faculty member on a formal and informal basis.
- Consider, if appropriate and necessary, the career of the new faculty member's partner and the special concerns which women faculty of child-bearing age may have.

Another relatively small department at Colorado State operates with a well understood and accepted informal procedure, now in place for many years. Selection of new faculty members has been unanimous, and, consequently, the whole faculty considers itself, in the words of the department chairperson, "to have a stake in the success of junior faculty." Hence, the attitude is one of collective mentoring even though a senior faculty member is designated by the chairperson to have specific mentor responsibility.

**Institutionally Mandated Approach.** East Carolina University reports the preparation of a university-wide plan for mentoring, and the proposed plan will proscribe a minimum program to be adapted to the needs of each college and its departments. Departments will have to have a plan, but, as proposed, participation in the program by individuals will be voluntary both on the part of the new faculty member and the mentor. This plan does not mandate departmentally based mentoring, as the mentor can be either from the department or from outside the department, and it will be coordinated with a variety of other university-wide activities for new faculty. Again, one might speak of a "mentoring system," reflecting the recommended principles of a good mentoring program.

Existing departmental programs at East Carolina include a program in the School of Art that provides each new faculty member with two mentors: one in the same studio area, who focuses with the mentee on the teaching relationship, and the other of whom is the school's dean. The Department of Political Science at East Carolina University has prepared and accepted as a department a written description of voluntary mentoring in which the chairperson selects the mentor. The plan is not a written part of the departmental code, however, but instead a departmental procedure. It is very extensive and includes explanations of the "Purpose," the "Administration of the Program," and the "Roles and Responsibilities" of the new faculty member, the mentor, and the chairperson of the department. The description of the expectations for both mentor and mentee is quite detailed and includes the preparation of a professional growth plan for the new faculty member. In addition there is a non-legally-binding statement of agreement and understanding to be signed by both mentor and mentee. The introductory paragraph of this agreement reads as follows:

> We are voluntarily entering into a mentoring relationship which we expect to benefit both of us and East Carolina University. We want this to be a rich and rewarding experience with most of our time together being spent

on substantive developmental activities. We will attempt to abide by the general guidelines of the mentoring program and fulfill our respective roles and responsibilities. We understand that the intended duration of the relationship is for two or three academic years, but reserve the option to dissolve the mentoring relationship at any time. To clarify each other's expectations and better plan for the current year, we have agreed upon the following items. [Department of Political Science, 1993, n.p.]

The above systems illustrate the two different systemic principles, namely, an institutionally encouraged and an institutionally mandated departmentally based program. In a time of systemic complexity both of these systems will work and promote more effective and purposeful mentoring than if the process is left to chance.

**"Do-Nothing" Approach.** Regrettably, there is a perception, perhaps based on reality, perhaps not, that a number of institutions and units within an institution do indeed do nothing. A recent book, which ought to be read by every new, tenure-track faculty member, entitled *Mentor in a Manual: Climbing the Academic Ladder to Tenure* by Schoenfeld and Magnan (1992), offers the following opinion: "Despite a recent movement to encourage the 'mentoring' of new hires by senior staff, three psychologists examining mentoring in actual practice have found that many departments continue to apply a form of *social Darwinism:* 'Let's throw the kids off the end of the pier and see whether they can swim or not. *We* didn't get any survival advice; why should *they?'* (p. 7). A negative, do-nothing approach is not what we need in the academy today as we become more attuned to the increasing need to nurture and preserve our human resources.

## Conclusion

If an institution wishes to introduce a planned and purposeful mentoring program, choices must be made. The first choice to be made is whether to mandate participation by unit. The institution must then choose whether to structure the program across disciplinary lines, within the department, or to mix both. Naturally, a choice also exists as to whether or not participation as mentee or mentor be voluntary or required; however, it is hard to imagine a successful program based upon required participation.

The degree of formalization of the program must also be decided, whether at the departmental or institutional level. At the department level, the choices are to adopt it as a formal part of a departmental code, as a written procedure, or as an unwritten procedure. Thus, one might speak of both formal and informal approaches, each of which could produce good results if the principles of effective mentoring are observed—purposeful and planned, reflective of institutional culture and departmental subculture, recognizing individual differences, responsive to needs and interests of the individuals involved, and flexible.

The benefits for mentor and mentee within the same department are, in the aggregate, no different from what they are in a relationship arising from a different context: encouragement to the new colleague to advance more quickly in professional understanding and accomplishment than without the mentoring relationship, a sense of renewal and excitement for the mentor, a synergism of energy, and more. A discipline-specific mentoring program in a department will encourage the new colleague's growth and development within that disciplinary context, and this, in turn, is essential for progress toward and ultimate attainment of tenure and promotion. The successful colleague, retained by the institution, is a manifestation of wise stewardship of institutional resources and of service to ourselves as persons.

## References

Boice, R. "Mentoring New Faculty: A Program for Implementation." *Journal of Staff, Program, and Organization Development,* 1990, *8,* (3), 143–160.

Boice, R., and Turner, J. L. "The FIPSE-CSULB Mentoring Project for New Faculty." *Improving the Academy,* 1989, *8,* 117–129.

Department of Food Science and Human Nutrition, Colorado State University. Departmental Code. (Used with permission.)

Department of Political Science, East Carolina University. Procedure adapted by the Department on Jan. 25, 1993. (Used with permission.)

Luna, G., and Cullen, D. L. "Mentoring Women and Minorities: Applications to Higher Education." *Journal of Staff, Program, and Organization Development, 10* (3), 133–139.

Roper, S. "A Mentoring System." In *Chairperson's and Department Head's Manual.* Office of Instructional Services, Colorado State University, 1989, rev., 1992.

Sandler, B. "Women as Mentors: Myths and Commandments." *Chronicle of Higher Education,* Mar. 10, 1993, p. B3.

Schoenfeld, A. C., and Magnan, R. *Mentor in a Manual: Climbing the Academic Ladder to Tenure.* Madison, Wis.: Magna Press, 1992.

*KAY U. HERR is associate director of the Office of Instructional Services at Colorado State University, Fort Collins, Colorado.*

*The need for mentoring does not end with new faculty orientation,*
*but continues throughout the careers of faculty members.*

# Mentoring Faculty for Midcareer Issues

*Daniel W. Wheeler, B. J. Wheeler*

Midcareer faculty face many issues that need to be confronted to move forward in their professional and personal lives. Many of these dilemmas and decisions can be facilitated by traditional mentoring as well as by other communication social support behaviors. This chapter identifies a number of midcareer issues and then examines some of the mentoring strategies that can be used to address them.

## Midcareer Issues

**Dealing with Career Disappointments.** A frequent career issue surfacing in the literature on the aging process is how middle-aged people deal with whether dreams or career expectations have been met (Gould, 1978; Levinson, Darrow, Klein, and McKee, 1978). Frequently these expectations are expressed in faculty consulting sessions where one hears statements such as this: "I thought my appointment at this institution was a temporary stop on the way to a more prestigious institution; now it looks like I will be here for the rest of my career." Anther concern may be lack of recognition or status: "I'm not going to make as big an impact in my field as I hoped." Both are variations on the theme of unmet expectations which require personal adjustments and development of more realistic expectations.

**Dealing with Specific Disappointments.** Not only are there the "macrodisappointments" concerning lack of career fulfillment, there are many "microdisappointments" that occur and, if not mediated in some fashion, these can lead to disengagement and cynicism. These disappointments or lack of successes can appear in at least two forms: The first concerns what are perceived to be broken promises and agreements. Faculty frequently express the view that commitments made by deans or department chairs have been broken. The faculty member believed, based usually on verbal agreements, that if he or she developed or completed a particular project or program, some reward or change in status would occur. We notice when working with these faculty members that incidents from the recent and distant past are often described as if they occurred last week. Many faculty need help to clarify these disappointments and put them behind them.

The second form of disappointment arises from what might be called unilateral contracts, which Partin (1991) describes as "unwritten, unspoken agreements between two parties—only one of whom knows of their existence" (p. 1). Partin further suggests that such contracts are "long on assumptions and short on mutual understandings" (p. 20). For example, a faculty member in a department may decide that relations with outside clientele need to be improved and so decides to take on the task of strengthening this alliance. The faculty member believes that he will be rewarded for these activities, but then later finds the department disappointed because it thought he should have been spending his time on research and writing. To prevent burnout caused by taking on too many tasks and faculty operating as "Lone Rangers," faculty need to be encouraged to present and gain departmental agreement on the importance of their activities before initiating them.

**Dealing with Career Plateauing.** Faculty often are faced with the issue of career plateauing or reaching a point where they sense they are not moving ahead (Bardwick, 1986). Two kinds of plateauing have been identified: "Subject matter plateauing" occurs when midcareer faculty members reach a point at which they believe they know what they need to know and have few subject matter challenges to address. They no longer find excitement in their subject. "Position plateauing" reflects the reality that faculty positions involve a short career ladder. A faculty member may become a full professor by age forty and sometime thereafter feel that there is no further level of advancement for which to strive. But advancement into an endowed professorship or a shift into administration may be possible. If these are not viable options, a faculty member may find a special program to coordinate or some new challenge that requires reaching out in a new direction. For example, the faculty member could coordinate a new general education program or take charge of another institutional initiative, such as retention, recruitment, or outreach. If none of these challenges are available, a faculty member may have to move to another institution to maintain a sense of career progress. In many plateauing situations, the need for a status change does not happen because many activities are seen as enrichment through new professional responsibilities.

**Adjusting to Changing Institutional Expectations.** Faculty members who continue at the same institution may experience a change in expectations and a consequent change in distribution of external rewards. The most frequent example concerns a faculty member who was hired with the expectation that teaching would be stronglying emphasized, then sometime later discovering that the institution now has higher expectations for research. These faculty members often express the opinion that "someone changed the rules." Some of these faculty never did research or have long since abandoned any research aspirations for a continuous effort on teaching and advising. In these situations, faculty either gear-up for research or find that those focusing on research glean most of the external rewards, while they are saddled with maintenance activities such as committee work, basic courses, and advising.

**Adjusting to Departmental Politics and Shifts in Power.** If one remains at an institution for a period of time, there are changes in the department such as turnover in administration, new faculty entering the department, and perhaps events that change the departmental focus. A faculty member may be a protégé under one chair's administration, and then be marginal or even on the outside with a new chair. Thus, a midcareer faculty member is constantly challenged to clarify his or her relationships and contributions to the department, and to consider new contributions suggested by the new departmental members and chair.

**Shifting into Administrative Role.** Faculty consider moving into an administrative role for a variety of reasons, such as enjoyment of the work, greater monetary reward, no one else available, belief they can do a better job, or a sense of wanting to try something new. This is often a difficult decision because of the potential consequences. Faculty complain that "I won't like it," "I will have to give up my discipline," or "My time will no longer be mine." With the present pattern of five to six years in department head positions (Seagren, Creswell, and Wheeler, in press; Carroll, 1991), unless the chair is continuing upward on an administrative track, most faculty will experience chairing as another assignment in their total repertoire of experience. These chairs need reflective counsel about the patterns possible, their strengths and weaknesses, and some useful resource people from whom to seek counsel.

**Preparing for a New Role Inside or Outside the Institution.** If a faculty member is preparing for a new role within the institution, there are usually professional development opportunities (sabbatical, study leave, change-of-duty station, professional development plan) to provide the temporary structure to allow the faculty member to reflect on these changes and retool to meet them. However, these changes, depending upon their magnitude (see Schuster and Wheeler, 1990) may take one to five years to achieve fully.

If the faculty member is moving outside higher education or to another higher education institution, major adjustments will be required, probably with little institutional help. One should keep in mind that these moves can be beneficial to both the individual and the institution. If a faculty member remains lost, without a sense of purpose and vitality, he or she can end up having a negative sense of self-worth, and thereby affect departmental morale. Thus, colleagues and sometimes administrators should provide the opportunity for the faculty member to clarify and explore how to move to the best situation, that is, to decide on the best career choice and how to maneuver the move.

**Coping with Dual Careers.** Whether there are more dual careers in academia today is unclear, but there certainly is a higher consciousness of issues involved in dual careers. There are conferences, offices in some institutions to help dual career couples, and often an explicit expectation by a job candidate that his or her spouse will be part of a "package deal." For a faculty member to consider a career move to another institution often requires determining whether there will be opportunities for the spouse or consideration of the effect on a long-range relationship. With a difficult job market because of hard economic times, the pressures on dual career faculty are intense. They require opportunities to discuss the most difficult professional and personal issues.

**Coping with Personal Issues.** When a faculty member begins a new position, energy and drive can seem unlimited. Career concerns and getting ahead seem more important than anything else. As time progresses and many faculty begin to address personal issues, their priorities can change. Personal issues may include personal health problems or those of the family or teenaged children or aging parents whose demands seem relentless. Marriage and financial concerns can invade her or his concentration. The efforts of the faculty member to address a myriad of professional and personal issues may sap the energy necessary to concentrate on one's career. Often this realization is precipitated by a specific event such as a family illness, a divorce, or a teenager getting into trouble. It can also be simply a growing sense of things out of control (see Creswell, Wheeler, Seagren, Egly, and Byer, 1990, chap. 9).

## Mentoring to Address Midcareer Issues

Considering the range of issues for midcareer faculty, it is easy to understand how faculty can become sidetracked or overwhelmed by conflicting choices. Mentoring in its various forms is one vehicle to assist faculty in addressing these career issues. Mentoring has a range of definitions, from the classic one of "an experienced adult who guides, advises, and supports inexperienced protégés for the purpose of furthering their careers" (Kroger-Hill, Bahniuk, and Dobos, 1986, p. 123) to someone who can "recognize the agenda of others and facilitate their progress" (Daloz, 1978, p. 24).

This chapter suggests that mentoring is a relationship in which a climate is created to address and sometimes even resolve professional and personal issues through support, advice, and challenge. The mentor may come from the ranks of department chairs and other administrators, junior and senior colleagues, colleagues at other institutions, colleagues from other disciplines, people from campus offices, spouse and children, friends, outside professionals (clergy, lawyers, and so on), students, and faculty organizations (unions, senates, and the like). One of the first mentors many faculty describe is their senior doctoral adviser or committee member. In short, mentors in the broadest sense can come from a wide range of people, associations, and organizations.

## What Mentors Do

**Colleague Mentoring.** Sands, Parson, and Duane (1991) believe that individual mentors can be of four types: (1) a friend, who provides friendship and emotional support; (2) a career guide, who provides collaboration in research or publications, introduction to persons who could further one's career, and involvement in professional networks; (3) an information source, who can highlight information about university policies and procedures, including promotion and tenure issues; and (4) an intellectual guide, who can provide intellectual guidance and review of academic products. Kram and Isabella (1985) suggest somewhat parallel peer relationships of (1) an information peer, for information sharing; (2) a collegial peer, for career strategizing and friendship; and (3) a special peer, for confirmation, emotional support, personal feedback, and friendship. These expanded conceptualizations of mentoring behavior suggest a wide range of behaviors and possibilities. No matter what the role or roles, the mentor relationship requires trust, frankness, and authenticity.

**Multiple Mentors.** Another mentoring model (Boice, 1991) suggests that faculty may have multiple mentors depending upon the academic functions in which they engage. Thus one might have a mentor in teaching, another one in research, and still another one in service. If mentoring is defined more in terms of learning specific skills and how to operate in a specialized area, then the multiple mentor approach is probably most effective.

Our observation is that a number of midcareer faculty who have outgrown or become distanced from their early adviser or mentor and have not found one at their present institution may find a new mentor by going outside the institution, often through a sabbatical experience. There is a close parallel between the role of the sabbatical mentor and the earlier adviser or mentor. Perhaps these are the conditions that lead to finding a mentor for many. The model for the relationship between a graduate student and a professor is that the expert helps the novice set goals and develop skills, and protects the novice, allowing risk and failure in a safe atmosphere and "facilitates the novice's successful entry into academic and professional circles and ultimately passes on his or her work to the protégé" (Hall and Sadler, 1983, p. 3).

A number of institutions have initiated a mentoring program or activity to help new faculty get started. However, even in the classic mentoring pattern of an established faculty member mentoring a new faculty member, Boice (1990) found that midcareer faculty can benefit from interaction with junior faculty, especially in the areas of research techniques and new paradigms. According to Shapiro, Haseltine, and Rowe (1978), this concept of "a continuum of helping functions among seniors, peers, and subordinates suggests that mentors who engage the protégé in the most intense and paternalistic relationship help shape and promote the novice's career and are in a position to intervene on the novice's behalf" (pp. 51–58).

**Group Mentoring.** Another form of mentoring can occur through group development. For example, at the University of Nebraska at Lincoln the Nebraska University Professional Renewal of Faculty Program (NUPROF) is specifically designed to help midcareer faculty reassess and refocus their careers. Faculty are placed in mini–support groups of three to four which cut across disciplines and personality types. Initially, groups are given activities designed to prompt communication and discussion of their careers. The expectation is that members will help each other work through the process of career refocusing, often requiring the resolution of some of the career issues presented in this chapter.

Although not all the groups have developed long-term mentoring with each other, some have continued their relationships long after the formal program ended. In one situation, the group has met monthly for lunch since 1984. One member is now retired and the other two have been at the university for ten to fifteen years. They have helped each other with their professional growth plans, sabbatical leaves, various professional and personal issues, and preparation for retirement. One of the group members suggests that this experience satisfies at least part of the need for collegiality. It's a time when the members can discuss any professional or personal issues. The key, he says, is the openness, the trust, and the willingness to exchange ideas and perspectives.

Another group began on an almost social basis. They did recreational activities, primarily fishing, together. However, as they were doing their sedentary fishing activity, they reflected on and discussed what was happening in their careers. One member of the group suggests that "The most powerful 'tool' I obtained from NUPROF was the formation and cultivation of the peer support group. This group has been instrumental in my own personal and professional development. The original support group still meets and functions regularly and serves a key role in planning" (Wheeler and Hartung, 1990, p. 12). All of this group have moved forward with strong new directions in their professional lives and continue to discuss issues and support each other.

Not all of the groups have been as successful, for a variety of reasons. Some of the reasons for lack of success include: unwillingness to commit to the relationship, lack of trust, inability to disclose information and feelings, and unwillingness to address significant aspects of work or life relationships. When commitment and trust in a relationship don't happen through normal interactions, they can be enhanced by a series of activities that invite discussion of various aspects of professional and personal life. These could include a group of questions, hypothetical situations, or goal clarification exercises.

Whatever their format, mentoring groups are committed to the development process and at least one of the group must be willing to initiate getting the group together. As one member of an ongoing mentoring group noted, "If Bill weren't willing to call us together, the group probably wouldn't meet."

Exactly what happens in the group can't be prescribed or mandated, but it can be planned or structured by group agreement. For more information on this program, see Lunde and Hartung (1990) in Schuster and Wheeler (1990).

## Conclusion

At this stage, maybe the most that can be concluded is that mentoring can play an important part in providing the means to resolve a number of important midcareer professional and personal issues. We do need more understanding of why and how it works and what situations can be developed to expand both the definitions and practices of mentoring throughout the faculty career.

## References

Bardwick, J. *Career Plateauing.* New York: Amacom, 1986.

Boice, R. "Mentoring New Faculty: A Program for Implementation." *Journal of Staff, Program, and Organization Development,* 1991 8, 143–160.

Carroll, J. "Department Chair Careers: A Call for Leadership." *Department Chair,* 1991, 2, 9.

Chronan-Hillix, Y. T., Chronan-Hillix, W. A., Gensheimer, L. K., and Davidson, W. S. "Students' Views of Mentors in Psychology Graduate Training." *Teaching of Psychology,* 1986, 13, (3), 123–127.

Creswell, J. W., Wheeler, D. W., Seagren, A. T., Egly, N. M., and Byer, K. D. *The Academic Chairperson's Handbook.* Lincoln: University of Nebraska Press, 1990.

Daloz, L. A. "Mentors: Teachers Who Make a Difference." *Change,* Mar.–Apr. 1983, pp. 24–27.

Gould, R. L. *Transformations.* New York: Simon & Schuster, 1978.

Hall, R. M., and Sadler, B. R. *Academic Mentoring for Women Students and Faculty: A New Look at an Old Way to Get Ahead.* Washington, D.C.: Association of American Colleges, 1983.

Kram, K. E., and Isabella, L. A. "Mentoring Alternatives: The Role of Peer Relationships in Career Development." *Academy of Management Journal,* 1985, 28, (1), 110–132.

Kroger-Hill, S. E., Bahniuk, M. H., and Dobos, J. "The Impact of Mentoring and Collegial Support on Faculty Success: An Analysis of Support Behavior, Information Adequacy, and Communication Apprehensions." *Communication Education,* 1989, 38, 15–33.

Levinson, D. J., Darrow, C. H., Klein, E. G., Levinson, E. B., and McGee, B. *The Seasons of a Man's Life.* New York: Knopf, 1978.

Lunde, J. P., and Hartung, T. E. "Integrating Individual and Organizational Needs." In J. Schuster and D. Wheeler (eds.), *Enhancing Faculty Careers: Strategies for Development and Renewal.* San Francisco: Jossey-Bass, 1990.

Partin, B. L. "The Unilateral Contract: A Faculty Morale Nightmare." *Department Chair,* 1991, 2 (2), 1,20.

Sands, R. G., Parson, L. A., and Duane, J. "Faculty Mentoring Faculty in a Public University." *Journal of Higher Education,* 1991, 174–193, 185.

Schuster, J. H., Wheeler, D. W., and Associates. *Enhancing Faculty Careers: Strategies for Development and Renewal.* San Francisco: Jossey-Bass, 1990.

Seagren, A. T., Creswell, J. W., and Wheeler, D. W. *The Department Chair: New Roles, Responsibilities and Challenges.* ASHE-ERIC Higher Education Report, in press.

Shapiro, E. C., Haseltine, F. P., and Rowe, M. P. "Moving Up: Role Models, Mentors and the 'Patron System.' *Sloan Management Review,* 1978, 19, 51–58.

Wheeler, D. W., and Hartung, T. E. "Views of NUPROF Participants." Unpublished manuscript, Office of Professional and Organizational Development, University of Nebraska, Lincoln, 1990.

DANIEL W. WHEELER is coordinator of the Office of Professional and Organizational Development and professor at the University of Nebraska, Lincoln.

B. J. WHEELER is assistant professor at Mississippi University for Women, Columbus.

# PART THREE

Personal Narratives of the
Mentoring Experience

*This chapter examines the graduate school experiences of three men of color who overcame significant obstacles in completing the dissertation writing phase of their program by initiating a peer mentoring group.*

# Peer Mentoring Among Graduate Students of Color: Expanding the Mentoring Relationship

*James Bonilla, Carlton Pickron, Travis Tatum*

Why should anyone interested in mentoring care to read about the experiences of three men of color as they struggled to complete their doctoral programs? Because higher education in America is in a real crisis. Colleges and universities across the nation are coming under increasing pressure to build faculties and student bodies that are reflective of the larger mosaic of American social diversity. Yet the most commonly cited reason for failing to recruit more faculty of color is that the pool of potential hirees to choose from is small. According to Magner (1993), institutions of higher education "end up stealing each other's minority scholars and battling for the few new minority doctorate holders who enter the job market each year" (p. A13). Magner also notes that African-Americans in 1982 earned 1,047 doctoral degrees, but in 1987 African-Americans earned only 768 (p. A13).

In a recent interview, Diane Ravitch, the outgoing assistant secretary of education, revealed that Latino dropout rates are nearly triple the national average ("Hispanics Have the Highest Dropout Rate," 1992). If the key to hiring more faculty of color is to enlarge the pool of minority doctorates, the implications of these trends are disturbing. Academia must develop an approach that recruits and retains students of color at the doctoral level or we risk a kind of American apartheid in higher education. Faculty will be increasingly white and students will increasingly be people of color unable to rise up the academic ladder of opportunity due to lack of academic credentials.

Expanding the pool of scholars of color has been the subject of considerable discussion in the last several years. One strategy put forth for increasing the presence of African-Americans at all levels of the university is faculty–student mentoring (Blackwell, 1989). Yet in his study of mentoring among African-American graduate and professional students, Blackwell found that only one in eight had a mentor who helped him or her with his or her career. He goes on to observe that part of the problem may be due to the low number of African-Americans in senior positions in education.

Kalbfleisch and Davies (1991) found that African-American professionals report having more mentors who are from their own ethnic group than from other cultural groups and that African-American professionals also report having more protégés who are from their own ethnic group than from other cultural groups. Yet in her 1989 article "Black and Female: Reflections on Graduate School," bell hooks recalls that "in all my years of studying in English department classes, I had never been taught by a black woman. In my years of teaching, I had encountered students in both English classes and other disciplines who had never been taught by black women" (p. 56). In predominantly white academia, a problem for many students of color, and certainly for the writers of this chapter, was finding mentors who were readily accessible from our own cultural groups.

Yet other problems also daunt students of color attempting to survive the doctoral ordeal. Arturo Madrid, director of the Thomas Rivera Center for Policy Studies on Latino Issues in San Antonio, Texas, states: "My experience, and this has been validated and confirmed, is that the highest attrition rates we experience in the Ph.D. granting process . . . is at the dissertation level. We have large numbers of Latinos who complete their programs of study, but never manage to complete their dissertations, which they need in order to move into the faculty ranks. . . . The principal reason is that Latinos have been at the margin of the Ph.D. granting process . . . and nobody looks after them once they are enrolled" (1993, p. 8). Not only do graduate students of color experience external dilemmas such as a lack of or ready access to mentors of color, but other issues persist. As hooks (1989) notes, "Racism and sexism are always present. . . . I talk with female black graduate students working in English departments. I hear many of the problems have not changed, that they experience the same intense isolation and loneliness that characterized my experience" (p. 61). Claude Steele (1992) elaborates on these issues of racial vulnerability and intense isolation in his article "Race and the Schooling of Black Americans": "From first grade onward, blacks have the extra fear that in the eyes of those around them their full humanity could fall with a poor answer or a mistaken stroke of the pen" (p. 75).

Thus a series of challenges face graduate students of color attempting to enter the realm of predominantly white academia. Few faculty of color are available for the necessary task of mentoring students of color. This lack contributes to a heightened sense of isolation and loneliness and racial vulnerability. And the ongoing struggle with intentional and unintentional acts of intolerance continues to play a role in discouraging the successful retention, especially at the dissertation phase, of potential future faculty of color. What, then, might we learn from the shared experiences of three graduate students of color, two African-Americans and one Puerto Rican?

In the winter of 1989 the three of us came together to support each other in the often painful process of completing our doctorates in education at the University of Massachusetts, Amherst, over a period of two years. Each of us came to the experience with successful careers in higher education (Carlton as an administrator, Travis as an assistant professor, and Jim as a national consultant in higher education). We also each brought master's degrees, the successful completion of our course work, and collective writers' blocks that were preventing us from moving forward into the writing phase of our doctoral work. As will become evident, we also shared a common sense of racial vulnerability, a lack of the traditional faculty–student mentoring relationship, and a subsequent lack of confidence in our academic abilities. In the following personal narratives, we revisit our educational roots to provide a context for our graduate student experiences, and consequently the role of traditional and peer mentoring.

## Personal Narratives of Peer Mentoring

**Jim.** My experience with European-American education began with my first year in school at the age of five. My mother (a single parent) had enrolled me in a Catholic school, a common practice among New York's two million Puerto Ricans in 1960. My mother worked, so my paternal grandmother, who spoke only Spanish, took care of me. Thanks to her, upon entering first grade I was bilingual, able to communicate both in English and in Spanish. However, that seemed to cause a problem and within months the nuns had summoned my mother to a conference about her son's "problem." According to them, I had a speech impediment (translation, "accent") and their "expert" advice was that I be placed in a class for children with learning problems. Hence by the age of six I had been labeled educationally different, and therefore was assumed to be deficient, because I spoke two languages.

Not surprisingly, I was kicked out of Catholic school at age nine due to disciplinary problems (stemming from my speech impediment, I suspect) and sent to a private reform school. While there I suffered a serious eye injury that left me legally blind and in need of special services only available through the New York City public schools. Mysteriously, my speech "impediment" disappeared the year I enrolled in public school.

I now realize that in many respects my eye injury in reform school was a turning point in my educational saga. While estimates are that 60–70 percent of Puerto Ricans in the New York City public schools drop out without receiving their high school diploma, I was not only able to shed the label of "speech-impaired," I shined as a student. This was due in part to the extra attention lavished on me by teachers due to my visual disability. In first grade, language had been used as an excuse to "disable" me. After my accident, I found that being blind afforded me educational opportunities such as extra time to take tests, access to extra tutoring, increased faculty attention, and a willingness on the part of many teachers to accept my difference as legitimate and tolerable.

While being a Puerto Rican with an accent had contributed to my being bounced out of Catholic school and into reform school, being blind eventually got me financial aid and off the streets of New York City and into a four-year state college in upstate New York. As one of fewer than thirty students of color (on a campus of 5,000), I would soon feel like an imposter in the temple. Routine jokes about Puerto Ricans stealing hubcaps and questions like "Do you take your knife to anatomy lab?" made it clear that my difference was not entirely understood or welcomed. Amid serious thoughts of dropping out in my sophomore year, I was given the opportunity to escape the hostility of this overwhelmingly white campus by being accepted to study abroad for my junior year. This became another turning point in my academic career. I was afforded an escape route and a new world literally opened up for this working-class, nineteen-year-old Nuyorican (New York Puerto Rican).

After receiving my bachelor's degree in education in 1976, I worked my way around the country with no thought of ever returning to the "ivory tower" of higher education. What eventually did entice me back to graduate school at the University of Massachusetts was a good friend and an innovative program that was exploring issues of racism, sexism, handicapism, and other forms of social oppression. Because of my life experience and prior work as a community organizer, I was accepted in 1984 and began my coursework toward my master's degree in the spring of 1985. That year was significant not only because I turned thirty, but also because it was the first time in my eighteen-year educational odyssey that I was given an opportunity to study the history of Puerto Ricans and the island of our origin. In addition, the program in which I was enrolled allowed me to take courses that were heavily experiential, oriented toward group learning, and highly participative in nature. My thirst for learning peaked and I literally found myself working well beyond the number of credits I needed to qualify for my degree.

At this juncture I made the decision to press on for the doctorate, reasoning that since my role model and adviser was an African-American and he had succeeded, and since I had already accumulated course credits that could be applied to the doctoral program, why waste the credits? Within a year of making the decision to enroll, I began to have second thoughts. This shadow of doubt became most acute when I confronted the reality that getting a dissertation was more than simply taking courses. It required original scholarship and, most terrifying of all, writing hundreds of pages. Incredible as it may seem, I had survived nearly eighteen years of education without having been required to write anything more substantial than a ten-page paper.

Many of my colleagues in the program were women who themselves were returning to the university and facing a similar crisis of confidence. I remember being particularly dumbstruck one day when I heard about a workshop for women entitled "Imposters, Frauds and Fakes: Women in Higher Education." I felt like an imposter, fraud, and fake as well! Sitting alone in front of the computer, struggling to compose a meaningful topic for my dissertation, I was seized by the sudden realization that all my life I had been regularly given mixed messages about my intellectual powers and my rightful place in the educational mainstream. Now I was preparing to enter into a process that would place me, a formerly legally blind, working-class Nuyorican, at the forefront of that same mainstream. To say I felt an overwhelming sense of fear is an understatement. For the next several months I found *something* to do, *anything* to do, rather than face the demons of my own self-doubt, racial vulnerability, and internalized oppression.

Faculty would sincerely try to be helpful. They would send me to writing seminars (full of white students) to encourage me to proceed. Because my African-American dissertation chair was often inaccessible, a white male committee member played a key role in providing me timely feedback on my manuscript. Still, the only way I can describe the vulnerability I felt is to point to the example of deer at night who are frozen in the headlights of an oncoming car—suddenly and terrifyingly revealed, their place of concealment torn away and their very safety in question. I was haunted by the internal fear that what I would write would be less than meaningless. It would be ridiculed as clearly a third-rate product of a person of color who stole his way into academe only because of affirmative action or some such device. Worse still, I was convinced that I alone felt this way until one day I ran across Carlton, an African-American classmate, in the library. In the process of talking about what was happening to us, we began to hold forth on our "writer's block." After hours of confession we became aware that "No, it wasn't just me," there were others like us, who shared our racial and cultural vulnerability and who were struggling to stay afloat. That night we agreed to call Travis, another African-American classmate, whom we both knew was also struggling, and arranged our first meeting.

Our initial group meetings consisted of relating to one another our experiences with writing and graduate school and being men of color. All three of us shared in common a dissertation committee chair who was African-American and all of us were struggling with our anger and our sense of vulnerability with being at a predominantly white institution. I recall just how much anger got released during those initial meetings and how they served to validate my experiences all the way back to first grade in Catholic school.

There was also a flavor and perspective to the group that was distinctly different from my interactions with white graduate students or faculty. Because the content of my dissertation directly involved racial issues, accurate and balanced reporting of the data was critical to establishing its trustworthiness and reliability. For example, I recall a meeting with a white faculty member on my committee who suggested that I had overquoted people of color in my study and underquoted white participants. Because of the power differential between me and him and because of my respect for his expertise, I was inclined to make changes in how I reported the data, but I first decided to ask for my support group's perspective. They unanimously felt that I had overquoted the white participants and underquoted participants of color. This caused me to tabulate exactly the number of times each participant group had been quoted and I was shocked to see that, in fact, I had quoted participants of color forty-eight times and white participants sixty-one times.

Another value of the mentoring group's existence for me was the regularity with which we met. Many of the demons I mentioned earlier made writing an especially difficult experience for me. While the reality of being at a predominantly white university and being faced with an occasionally hostile environment was not new, it did not prepare me for the internalized fear and racial vulnerability I experienced as I struggled with the writing of my dissertation. I often asked the question out loud, "What is a working-class, New York Puerto Rican trying to do entering the ivory tower?" While Carlton and Travis had each asked themselves the same question, they were unrelenting in their insistence on my right to be in that ivory tower. Their patience and understanding, as well as the fact that I felt safe expressing these emotions to them without worrying about how white colleagues would react, made a major difference in my ability to persevere. At each step of the process of writing the comprehensive exam, writing the dissertation proposal, and completing the dissertation itself they were as reliable a group of supporters as I could have hoped for. Often access to my committee chair was limited. At these times, a call to my peers was often all I needed to continue writing and overcome that particular day's writing block.

I was the first person in the group to take my comprehensive examinations, yet the last person to defend his dissertation. Both Carlton and Travis finished ahead of me. I owe much to the fact that they never once considered dropping out once their individual goals were reached. Two years after our first meeting I defended my dissertation and all three of us went on with our careers, now with doctorates in hand.

**Carlton.** My early school years weren't entirely smooth sailing. In about the fifth grade it became evident that my reading and writing skills weren't very good. In the eighth grade I developed a nervous stomach related to reading and writing issues. At that time I started meeting with a tutor, which helped a great deal. Looking back from my perspective today, I think I probably had an undiagnosed learning disability which over the years I learned to cope with. By the time I finished college with a "C" average from a highly demanding academic program, I hated school and the idea of a graduate degree was out of the question.

But after working as a teacher for two years, I realized that I could do a better job if I received further education. I was accepted into a graduate program with probationary status because my undergraduate grade point average was too low. That was okay with me: I just wanted to be accepted. I worked harder than I had ever worked before during the two years of this graduate program. I spent more time in the library during the first week of graduate school than I had spent in the library during my entire undergraduate career. I took this opportunity seriously and expected everyone around me to do the same. I didn't have time for weak professors or students and I had a few run-ins because of that. While there was no peer mentoring among graduate students, I did receive some mentoring from my adviser. Despite many obstacles, I persevered and graduated with an "A–" average.

Working in higher education, I saw the writing on the wall: get your doctorate degree. I often compare my doctoral courses to the running of a marathon. My 26.2 mile academic marathon was about to begin! I was accepted into a program where the course work was demanding and fulfilling and the learning environment enjoyable. This phase seemed like the "comfortable" first thirteen miles of the marathon.

The second phase of the marathon was more complicated and challenging. I needed to write my comprehensive exam, propose a dissertation topic, conduct my research, and have my dissertation topic accepted. This was all too overwhelming. I had a two-year period of little to no activity on my degree. During this time I changed my topic, lost my drive to finish, lost direction, suffered from no advising, and consequently doubted my ability to write the dissertation. I did not want to see any of my committee members; I did not want to associate with university colleagues at all. I started looking for a way out with dignity, but there was no way out without the degree. Faced with this reality, I went to the library and sat there for three hours and produced half an outline. I remember breaking down and crying while driving home. Meeting with a colleague who was also a personal friend, I again broke down and cried, but this time I was able to get some feedback about what I was experiencing and feeling. This was the beginning of the end—the sixteen-mile marker of the marathon. I was able to complete my outline.

Work was progressing but I needed some feedback from my committee chair; that became the next challenge. He was a hard person to connect with; our relationship had always been distant. The lack of connection and direction started to anger me and slow me down. Back in the library I ran into Jim, a fellow doctoral student and friend. We began to talk about our experiences with the academic process. He suggested getting together. I called another friend, Travis, to see if he wanted to meet with the two of us. Thus our peer mentoring group was formed.

I was resistant in the early meetings because I was unable to get what I wanted from my chairperson. I questioned the process, the degree, and myself once again. The group was great—it allowed me to vent my anger. I had two other people who could respond to what I was dealing with from their two different perspectives. It felt good to be heard and to get feedback. The first two or three meetings dealt with my anger. After these meetings, my writing became smoother and I became more productive. My mind was set: I determined to finish my degree and not let anyone stop me. I also had visions that I might die before I finished and that thought really enraged me! So I prayed to God not to let it happen. Now I was passing the twenty-mile marathon marker. I knew I would finish.

The group served as a forum for me to vent my frustrations, get feedback, gain insight, and attain direction and guidance in a safe environment. It was an environment that let me be myself without any concern for what was being said or to whom. Bouncing ideas off one another as peers was productive. An unexpected positive feature of the group was that we were in three different phases of our doctoral program. Jim was finishing up his comprehensive exams, I was just starting mine, and Travis was finishing up his course work and starting to talk about his comps. Our conversations were active, with each of us sharing our experiences and strategies for continued progress. For example, assisting Jim as he prepared for his comprehensive exams and attending his exam defense was uplifting. I was able to see that passing comprehensive exams was an achievable goal and the experience reinforced my belief that I too would succeed. Another type of feedback and guidance that we were able to offer each other dealt with completing the different forms required at each stage of the doctoral process. We discussed how to manage our committees as well as how to manage our lives outside the doctoral process. A student's personal life impacts greatly on what work gets done and how sanity is maintained. In my case, I was able to explain to my wife how she could best help and support me.

The group also helped me with my relationship with my chair. Looking back, I can see that he was a role model, not a mentor. I looked up to him, admired his accomplishments, and learned a great deal in his classes. However, our relationship did not evolve into a mentoring one. During the exit interview I explained my feelings to my chairperson and felt that our discussion was productive. The last form was signed and I crossed the finish line of the marathon.

Being in an active, motivated, committed, and supportive group was one key to the success I experienced. Having people to lean on, to push me to do my work, to encourage and respond to my personal growth, was critical. The group was also able to help me make meaning of my doctoral work and how it fits into my life.

**Travis.** Of all the factors that have influenced my educational experience, the one that stands out for me is that I am the first generation from my family to achieve this level of education. I continue to view my background as black and working class, and this has had an impact on how I have experienced education. On the one hand, my family really wanted me to get an education. They always thought that education was important and supported my desire for higher education with all the resources they had available. On the other hand, the length of my educational experience and ambiguity concerning the meaning of the outcome was sometimes a source of tension for them and for me. There was concern on their part as to what kind of job my education would lead to and when. As for me, I was not always clear as to the ends of the process. I could not say what job a graduate education would lead to or what my own goals were in terms of a doctoral degree. I did know that I enjoyed the learning experience. And one of the issues that made the experience worthwhile for me was the emergence of a black identity and the need to come to terms with that identity and what it meant. This level of abstraction was not a comfort to my family.

In addition, the issue of being black in academia is significant because of the ways in which the academy deals with black intellectual development. On more than one occasion I noted the surprise on professors' and students' faces when I indicated that I had read and understood material. Perhaps the surprise resulted from the fact that I am black and had been an athlete, so that there was an expectation that I would not understand some ideas and concepts. Here, too, was a point of struggle in which it was necessary to come to terms with my sense of self and my own sense of self-doubt. Having come from a working-class background and being black meant that I did not always feel at home in the academy. Did I belong? And perhaps more importantly, could I do the work? There was a definite sense of being an alien in the environment. Although I am still in academia, that sense of being an alien has not completely disappeared.

One of the things that helped me survive the experience was the fact that I was able to find mentors, black professors, who were willing to take the time to talk about intellectual work, to explain the process for accomplishing that work, and to model a strong sense of self as black people. These mentors were brilliant in their academic work and they were able to connect the work to their experience and give it meaning for me. This was done through an ongoing process of dialogue, much of it outside of class, in which meaning was created and shared. I did not have the experience of this kind of depth with white professors, so this process made a difference for me.

Because I was involved with two graduate programs, one at the University of Michigan, and one at the University of Massachusetts, I have had two slightly different experiences with mentoring by black professors. My experience at the University of Michigan was powerful because of the intellectually challenging environment that was present there at the time. Both faculty and students were engaged in numerous, intense debates about the social issues of the 1970s. Because my mentor and other junior faculty were allied with graduate students in questioning and challenging the fundamental assumptions underlying the social structures of society, including the university itself, these professors did not last long at the university. Within three years or less most were gone.

The loss of this relationship with professors with whom I identified cut me off from and aborted a process that I was only beginning to understand. While I had the option to leave with my mentor, I made the decision to stay at the university under the false assumption that I could move through the dissertation process alone. I did not fully understand the process, even though I felt that I could meet the challenge inherent in it in spite of, or perhaps because of, all the political turmoil during those first years. It took several years to understand my own isolation and marginality in the doctoral process.

Another mentoring experience that was necessary and useful to me was the development of a peer mentoring group that included a black and a Latino graduate student. This group became a source of further information about the dissertation process, an opportunity to share experiences, and an impetus to work on areas in which each of us had weaknesses and needed support. One of the main areas of our concern was writing.

In the mentoring group, we could bring our work to the group for feedback. The group could give an individual the needed push to overcome any blocks he might have experienced.

Another useful aspect of the peer mentoring group was that it involved a process in which the members felt a sense of authenticity about our feelings, our professors, the doctoral process, and our writing. We could communicate with each other and share our experiences and feelings without worrying about each other's reactions or misunderstanding where those feelings were coming from. This was useful because it acted as a stimulus to keep working and moving forward. We were all working full time, had families or significant relationships, and were doing graduate work. The mentoring group became an important alternative to the isolation that many graduate students experience.

This experience led me to conclude that the mentoring process was very important to my success in graduate school. Moreover, I came to realize the importance of a mentoring process that focuses not only on the content but also on the process of intellectual life in academia. My faculty mentoring experiences have been significant in terms of my own intellectual growth, but my peer mentoring experience at the University of Massachusetts was more intense and useful in terms of completing the degree because it dealt with the process of surviving in academia. There were lengthy discussions of how academia functioned, how to be engaged in the process, how to write analytically, how to seek feedback from the process, and an opportunity to participate in the writing of an article. My guess is that many white graduate students have mentors who provide this kind of support. What is not clear to me is whether or not these kinds of opportunities are available for black and other minority students who are perceived as being marginal or who feel that they are marginal. Clearly the process of completing my doctoral program was facilitated by such an experience.

## Reflections on Advantages of Peer Mentoring Approach

The peer mentoring group had a number of advantages for us that were helpful to us in completing the doctoral process.

• The group met regularly every two to three weeks. This was important because the regular meetings kept people on task and focused on both short- and long-term deadlines.

• The group was an important source of feedback about our writing, our research, and our thinking on problem areas with dissertations. The feedback process was facilitated by the fact that we felt that the group offered a safe environment for the sharing of information and comments on each other's work. Because we were all people of color there was an openness in the group. We were free to make comments and hear comments without feeling defensive about what was said or second guessing what was meant.

• We were free to be authentic and to reveal or to vent our feelings. This process of venting included feelings of anger, frustration, and sometimes fear and racial vulnerability. In this process there was validation and affirmation of our sense of self and entitlement to succeed. Having the opportunity to vent these feelings provided the basis for academic and personal growth. By doing so, we integrated the graduate experience into our real lives. We could put the process in perspective in terms of our families and our working selves.

• The group provided direct support in the preparation for comprehensive examinations and dissertation proposals. We attended each other's exams to see how the process worked and to provide support for each other. This was an important feature of the experience. While exams and defenses are public events, very few, if any, graduate students bother to attend them. Yet attending these events provides valuable insights into how the process actually works.

• The group provided valuable information on how to go through the doctoral process. We shared information on how to choose, manage, and negotiate with a committee so that relations remained positive. We learned how to write proposals and dissertations in the proper style mandated by the university, what forms to complete, and which secretaries to see and which to avoid. While some of these points may appear minor, they can make a big difference in terms of how smoothly someone moves through the experience.

• The group members who had finished their dissertations continued to meet with the group until all members had finished.

• This group deliberately remained small and did not admit new members once it had solidified its core membership. This may be one reason why members continued to support each other until all had finished. It did not have to go through the process of redefining itself every time new members came in or old members left.

## Summary and Implications

In our collective experience with the mentoring process it is important to differentiate between a peer mentoring group and the traditional faculty–graduate student mentoring relationship. While both types of mentoring relationships have something to offer graduate students, there are significant differences between the two. The major difference lies in the power and status relationship of the faculty–student relationship versus the equality inherent in the peer mentoring relationship.

The power and status in the faculty–student mentor relationship is important. Students need this kind of hierarchical relationship because it recognizes that the faculty person has some expertise and knowledge that can be passed on to the student. For the faculty mentor, it is not simply an issue of having more power than the student, but of using that power and influence to assist the student whenever there are problems and conflict in the process of getting the degree. Sometimes the faculty mentor can use his or her power, prestige, and influence to gain access to research funds for the mentee, or to support the mentee's publications, or to fund the mentee's presentations at professional conferences. Also, the mentor can offer the mentee an opportunity to collaborate on research work. All these activities become part of the process of moving a student through the doctoral maze as well as helping him or her to make sense of the academic culture and its underlying assumptions.

While the traditional faculty–student mentoring relationship can certainly be beneficial for the student, it is based on inequality. The student remains the subordinate. Even when the student reaches the same degree level, he or she will still remain in a deferential relationship to the mentor given the roles they have played with each other.

However, in a peer mentoring relationship the situation is very different. Students meet as equals and are free to interact and communicate without any need to defer to each other. Both relationships have advantages and can work well together in moving students through a long and difficult process. Indeed, by employing both a faculty–student mentoring process and a peer mentoring process it may be possible to move students through a graduate program more quickly, to contribute to personal growth, and to validate racial identity.

Part of the solution to opening the academic pipeline for faculty of color must include strategies for mentoring graduate students of color successfully. Our collective experience suggests that a peer mentoring group can have a positive impact on a graduate experience and can assist students in completing a terminal degree. This we believe to be true for all students, but especially for students of color, who may be more marginal and have less access to traditional mentors and support systems.

### References

Blackwell, J. "Mentoring: An Action Strategy for Increasing Minority Faculty." *Academe*, 1989, 75, 8–14.

Deitz, R. "Tomas Rivera Center: Teacher Training and Education Policy." *Hispanic Outlook in Higher Education*, 1993, 3 (8), 6–9.

"Hispanics Have the Highest Dropout Rate, ED Says." *Black Issues in Higher Education*, Oct. 8, 1992, p. 4.

hooks, b. "Black and Female: Reflections on Graduate School." In b. hooks, *Talking Back: Thinking Feminist, Thinking Black.* Boston: South End Press, 1989.

Kalbfleisch, P., and Davies, A. "Minorities and Mentoring: Managing the Multicultural Institution." *Communication Education,* 1991, *40,* 266–271.

Magner, D. "Duke U. Struggles to Make Good on Pledge to Hire More Black Professors." *Chronicle of Higher Education,* Mar. 24, 1993, p. A13.

Steele, C. "Race and the Schooling of Black Americans." *Atlantic Monthly,* Apr. 1992, pp. 68–78.

*JAMES BONILLA is director of the Multicultural Teaching Program in the Center for Teaching Excellence at The Ohio State University, Columbus.*

*CARLTON PICKRON is associate dean of academic affairs and director of academic advising at Westfield State College in Westfield, Massachusetts.*

*TRAVIS TATUM is assistant professor of education at Westfield State College in Westfield, Massachusetts.*

*Foreign students in American universities can acquire cultural understanding and increase self-discovery through the support of mentors and cultural guides.*

# Taking a Cultural Journey Through Mentorship: A Personal Story

*Virgie O. Chattergy*

It would be an understatement to say that my life changed forever when I left my home country, the Philippines, to pursue graduate studies at the University of California at Los Angeles (UCLA). Those six years of student life were like sailing on a ship that stopped at many shores and weathered many different seas. I learned how to be a student in one place, then had to learn how to be a student all over again in a different place. There were enough similarities in my two different experiences to help me survive. But there were also enough differences to make me question my perceptions of, and expectations about, higher education and my abilities to succeed. The mentoring I received helped in this journey of cultural and self-discovery.

This reflection focuses on the many forms that mentoring takes. I believe that when dealing with international students, it may be more effective to go beyond the traditional mentoring formats to consider other aspects involved in adjusting to different cultural systems and norms. Often, mentoring is more of an attitude than a process. Formal mentoring programs are an asset to an institution, but all members of the university faculty and staff can be taught to see themselves as mentors, guides, and advocates for the students they encounter in the course of their work. My own journey is a commentary on how effective mentoring by various people combined to provide a rich growth experience.

## Cultural Mentoring: First Port of Call

A heightened sense of awareness about cultural differences developed that first year in the United States, and with it, my appreciation for the assistance extended to foreign students. Although I did not know the word then, "mentoring" was provided by faculty and support staff of a newly developed UCLA program enrolling students representing about forty countries. Through my participation in this program, I became part of a formal mentoring network. The most important function of the mentoring aspect at this stage was advice about practical matters. For a foreign student, the first weeks in a new country are a crucial adjustment stage when the student has a critical need for help from counselors and mentors. For instance, we were told about always checking to make sure we were waiting in the correct line so we did not end up wasting precious hours. We were taught how to find our way around campus, where to go to buy groceries, and where the nearest Catholic church was located. I didn't get much help with my academic program or get cues about how to interact with my professors. Because I wasn't part of a cohort of students identified with a particular program, I had less access to the professors and to the process of understanding the complex academic traditions and culture of the American university.

My first serious problem erupted the first week after I arrived. Not having had an orientation to the university, I was surprised to discover the enormous out-of-state tuition fee required for registration. No one had walked me through the forms. If anyone were to ask me what initially struck me as different about being a student in the United States, I would have to answer "Filling out forms." Sure, I knew about forms, but I was not prepared to cope with all the forms I had to fill out at registration. The "mentor" used to tease us with the warning, "Remember, now, if you pass registration successfully, you're over 50 percent of the hurdle." Had it not been for a quick-thinking, sympathetic registrar on the other side of the desk, I don't know what might have happened to me. The registrar asked for my application forms and said she would be back shortly. Ten long minutes later she returned. Handing me back the forms, she said that based on my immediate past scholarship, my tuition would be waived, but I would have to maintain a certain grade point average for the waiver to carry over to the next semester. This form of mentoring will occur naturally if student services personnel see themselves as an important link in the adjustment of new students. Mentoring requires the ability to see the situation from the learners' perspective and to provide needed coaching and guidance.

My lack of familiarity with certain "protocols" of classroom interaction resulted in an unfortunate experience with a professor who had different expectations concerning my performance. A bit of background information may be helpful here. English had long been my second language when I began my graduate studies. From kindergarten through college I attended a private girls' school in which English was the medium of instruction. I had been teaching in the same college when I decided that I needed more training in the general area of pedagogy and in the particular field of teaching English as a second language (ESL).

Students in the ESL certificate program were tested to assess their levels of knowledge and ability in various aspects of English. My reading ability and grammatical competence on a pencil-and-paper test were rated superior. My speaking ability in English was also rated very highly. My overall test score was 96 over 100. Ironically, the results of my assessment test worked against me. I had always been only slightly above average as a student, with no compelling ambition to strive for higher ranking. I spent more time on extracurricular activities than I did on homework: glee club, social action groups, drama club. I've always believed that scores don't tell the whole story about one's education. I carried this same attitude into graduate work.

The quantitative score I received, however, generated high expectations from my professor. When I failed to meet her expectations, she concluded that I was not a serious student. When I failed to receive an A on a paper that had no comments written on it other than "Succinct," I tried subtly to impress upon her that unless she really believed my paper was of B quality based on some criteria applied to every paper, I would appreciate a re-evaluation because a scholarship was riding on the grade. She then reprimanded me for not spending more time in the library or study hall, where she often saw her other students. I had grown up with the belief that students never challenged their professors, and I was too new to the U.S. system of higher education to cross that cultural barrier in spite of what was at stake.

A positive experience in mentoring by another professor had a different outcome. At a midterm test in a class on syntax, I was puzzled at the simplicity of parts of the test. I completed the test in record time. However, when the tests were returned to us, I discovered that I had scored barely enough points to pass. Stunned, I went over the test while the professor was standing by my chair. He said, "I too am very surprised. See me after class." I appeared at his door feeling confused, angry, and utterly frustrated. Confused because the objective part of the test was where I missed points and these items dealt with punctuation marks. I missed placing periods in seven out of ten sentences. Angry because I felt insulted at having to take such a ridiculously low-level type of test. Frustrated because by this time, the aura of "newness" to the place had begun to wear off and I couldn't see what I was learning from these courses. I had left friends and a successful teaching career behind me for a supposedly enriching and challenging experience abroad. In short, I was full of self-pity and self-recriminations for not having paid attention to details.

The professor took one look at me and said, "Let's take a walk." Outside in a very informal setting, sitting on the grass, he listened patiently as I poured out my unhappiness. I don't remember what was said but I do recall feeling satisfied that he listened to me. This professor was originally from Canada. I have often wondered if his sensitivity to how I felt because I had left my home far behind evoked special sympathy because he too had experienced a sense of loss and loneliness. We never talked about his cross-cultural experiences, but as a mentor he went beyond his classroom obligations to support a student struggling with cultural barriers.

This interaction became a turning point in my attitude. After that I tried to see most things as if I were seeing them for the first time. I also decided not to assume too much, including not to assume that people knew me and recognized my abilities without my having to prove myself. I found out years later when the same professor came to Hawaii for a conference that he too remembered that afternoon. How could he forget, he said, when after that conversation with me, he never gave that type of an exam again. It turned out that it was required by the director as part of his idea of assessing students' growth in learning the English language, a mistaken notion. This encounter illustrated the value of mentoring that contributed to the growth of both parties.

In retrospect, I believe that some of the difficulties I experienced were due to a combination of my status in the program, my expectations versus those held by the professors, and my propensity to be self-sufficient and independent, which did not fit the stereotypical image that the professors had concerning Filipino students. The value of mentoring is often diminished if cultural values and beliefs are not identified as part of the relationship.

## Becoming Bicultural: Enriching Experiences

During the mentoring process, I was reminded that cultural expectations are often unspoken and misunderstood. For instance, supposedly Filipinos don't generally ask questions, nor do they banter, but I did both. Looking back on it now, I firmly believe as I did then, that mentoring needed to go both ways—students need mentoring about schooling in the host culture and staff need mentoring about students and their sociocultural backgrounds. Filipinos *do* ask questions and *do* banter, but not with authority figures, only among their equals. In a social context with adults I generally consider everyone equal. Perhaps I misinterpreted American informality for camaraderie. In fact, for some time now it has been apparent to me that in the eyes of some people, Filipinos will never be accepted as equals because of their former colonial status. They are not viewed as "inferior," but as "not equal." It's like never being treated as a grown-up in some parent–child relationships because the once-in-charge adult cannot or will not shift his or her role. Furthermore, when I need to know something, I ask. In neither instance did I believe I was being non-Filipina, though I may not have fit other people's stereotype of Filipinos.

As a Filipina, I was socialized into conventions and mores that were part of being a student. For example, Filipinos stop whatever they are doing and stand up when a professor walks in. This is a sign of respect. In the United States I did this for a couple of weeks and totally confused my professor, who would look at me quizzically while I responded with a smile. He'd look down and shake his head slightly. So I got the point. My nonverbal reaction to what

I thought was a cue to demonstrate my respect for him was irrelevant. For all I know, the behavior may have been downright annoying to him.

Raising my hand to "get the floor" or to be called upon was another ritual I brought to America from the Philippines that did not serve me well in seminar classes. A professor, familiar with behavior patterns in Philippine classrooms, told me to just speak up or I'd never get a word in.

Perhaps the most powerful cultural dimension of mentoring that needs to be learned early is the way we communicate, verbally and nonverbally. Initially, I tended to give lengthy answers to the greeting "How are you?" until I realized that the faculty member was not really asking a question but simply making a friendly greeting that did not require a complex answer. It didn't take long to realize that knowledge of the language was useful, but not always helpful. Cultural messages are embedded in language. I had to learn that while dictionaries give definitions of words, people give them other meanings and connotations that convey a message which escapes literal translation. Filipinos rely heavily on nonverbal signals and responses. Whenever I called someone from a distance with a hand gesture, the person would wave back. The way Filipinos use the hand movement for calling someone over is the American's way of waving good-bye. Filipinos also tend to give directions with an accompanying head movement. They tilt their heads toward the direction indicated and they press and purse their lips with this gesture. It took an ex–Peace Corps volunteer in the Philippines to tell me that for Americans and possibly for other non-Pacific folks, I was suggesting a kiss. That ended the habit.

In remembering those years, it has become apparent to me that mentoring occurred at many different levels and in a variety of contexts. The most effective mentoring actions for me were those that happened informally and in circumstances when I was interacting with an individual or within a small group setting and my unique ethnic, gender, and cultural characteristics were understood and valued.

## Informal Mentoring: Outside the Institution

To supplement my meager allowance from home and small part-time pay, I lived with an American family in exchange for babysitting duties. The couple considered themselves very liberal, which they explained meant they were very accepting of people of other cultures and races. Most of all, they saw themselves as friends of foreign students. They became mentors through their commitment to providing opportunities to students adjusting to American culture. They made it a practice to help students like myself who needed a break in making both ends meet. The mother didn't work, although she had graduated from a major university with a master's degree. As a housewife, she enjoyed cooking the family meals. She took pride in teaching me how to prepare simple American dishes and to appreciate coffee: "You have not really become an

American until you learn to drink coffee—black," she'd say with a wink. (I did learn to appreciate coffee but cannot drink it without cream and sugar.) Around the dinner table, the father would ask the children to share something about their day. Each child was given some time to speak and often the youngest one had to be reminded to wait her turn or wrap it up when she went over time. I found this pattern of interactive behavior reflected in the schools that I observed.

Following my earlier established pattern of spending as much time off-campus as on, I became quite active in the international students' association. While my peers spent weekends fixing meals that reminded them of home and talked in their native language, I was refining my schwa sounds that are so challenging to the Filipino-formed tongue. My living arrangement was one of the reasons I couldn't be in the library in the late afternoons, but it was complicated to explain to the professor who had already implied that I was not a serious student. On some Sundays I'd spend a good part of the day with other Filipino UCLA students and through them would further enlarge my circle of acquaintances when I was introduced to their friends. Furthermore, because I had to take a forty-five minute bus ride to and from campus, I made friends with the regulars on the bus. One woman in particular opened her house to me so that I met the family often and was welcomed into her home for important holidays. I still remember vividly the first Thanksgiving dinner I attended at her house. I gained another level of understanding about the festivity and it ceased to be an abstract idea I read about only in books and magazines.

From these social and personal interactions, I was able to discuss my academic concerns. I interacted with students outside of my field and learned about other scholars' approach to their work. For instance, through my friendship with a West Indian sociology major, I had opportunities to attend and meet some actors in local theaters, for he was researching some aspects of their careers. He took me along to record the interviews he had set up. From him, I saw the world through yet another pair of eyes.

Although the idea of mentoring was not consciously in my mind or in theirs, my interactions with other students and families during those years, in effect, were passages into cultural streams with mentors guiding me even as I influenced some in my journey from one place to the next. Given my reflections, I'd say that, although it wasn't always smooth sailing, there were not as many rough waters to cross as there could have been. My journey continues and I can now mentor others as well.

*VIRGIE O. CHATTERGY is professor of curriculum and instruction and interim director of the Center for the Study of Multicultural Higher Education at the University of Hawaii, Manoa.*

*In this personal narrative a West Indian reflects on her culture and her graduate mentoring experiences in the American academic environment at a predominantly white university.*

# Mentoring Minority Graduate Students: A West Indian Narrative

*Christine A. Stanley*

In July 1980, at the age of sixteen, after I graduated from high school in Kingston, Jamaica, the West Indies, I pursued undergraduate studies in Texas. In September 1983, after completing baccalaureate studies with honors at Prairie View A&M University, I was accepted into the master's degree program in the Department of Biology at Texas A&M University. After obtaining my master's degree, I entered the doctoral program in the Department of Educational Curriculum and Instruction and successfully completed this degree in November 1989. I recount these academic accomplishments because, on reflecting about the mentoring experiences that I had in graduate school, I have come to realize that each tier of the academic ladder marks a different level of experience in the mentoring process.

I remember all too clearly the day of my interview and visit with prospective advisers for the master's degree program in zoology in the Department of Biology at Texas A&M University. Dr. William P. Fife was my last visit on the itinerary that had been prepared for me. He pushed back his chair, put his hands behind his head, looked across his desk at me, and asked, "What do you want out of life, Christine?" After I told him about my short-term goals and my long-term goal, which at that time was to be a physician, he went on to inquire about my areas of interest, to probe my strengths and weaknesses, and to explain how he and the department faculty could assist me in achieving my goals. We discussed the differences in the campus environment, for Texas A&M was a predominantly white institution and Prairie View was a historically black institution, in addition to the quality and climate of the department. He explained that, though the university was improving in terms of its recruitment efforts, the enrollment of black students was low.

The total enrollment at Prairie View was approximately 5,000, while at Texas A&M it was approximately 39,000 students. Dr. Fife further explained that, as compared to Prairie View, there was not a wealth of social support systems in place, and the department had enrolled only a few black students. In fact, I think I was the second black student and the first black female to obtain a graduate degree in the department. He made the situation very clear to me, saying, "I don't ever want to see you walking around here with your head held down, like you don't belong. Be confident about yourself and about what you are doing." Apparently he had observed this behavior in other minority students and recognized their feelings of isolation; he wanted to make sure that I did not experience the same thing. He further emphasized that Prairie View, even though a part of the Texas A&M university system, was not Texas A&M, and Texas A&M was not Prairie View: He warned me that I might experience periods of maladjustment. This, however, was not a problem for me. Being from a racially diverse country and having attended a racially diverse high school in Jamaica, the only maladjustment I experienced was getting accustomed to the size of the institution. That day, in Dr. Fife's office, was the beginning of my graduate mentoring experience.

Based on my areas of interest and his disciplinary expertise and experience, we mutually decided that Dr. Fife would be my graduate adviser. Of all the potential professors that I had interacted with, I appreciated him most for his warmth, candor, and wisdom. He made me feel relaxed. One of the professors that I interviewed asked, "Why do you want to come here? Why not go to Howard University?" To this day, the only reasons that I can think of for him to say such a thing to me were either his desire to spare me what he thought would be an uncomfortable learning experience, or his belief that I could not succeed in that environment. I never asked him why he said these things. I did not want to know and I really did not care. I had more important things to worry about.

The most significant characteristics that I appreciated in Dr. Fife were his overwhelming confidence in my abilities, his belief in my potential for success, and his role in shaping me as a professional. Perhaps even more intrinsically important was his ability to provide me with sincere, concrete, and honest feedback during my years as a graduate student in the Department of Biology. Whenever I did not perform up to my potential, he would give specific, constructive suggestions for improvement. I remember applying to various medical school programs in Texas and being offered several interviews. While Dr. Fife supported me wholeheartedly in this endeavor, he also told me to keep my options open, as I had several other skills and talents that I might want to give attention to as well. Another incident comes to mind: When I was thinking of scheduling my master's thesis defense, he told me candidly, "You can go ahead if you think that you are ready, but I really don't think you are." Dr. Fife took me "under his wing," and gave me opportunities for intellectual, academic, social, and personal growth. He helped to lay the foundation for the start of a graduate degree program, while at the same time allowing me room for independence.

It was during the two years in this program, and under his tutelage, that I was given the opportunity to be a teaching assistant in a human physiology course taught by him, to coauthor a laboratory manual, and be a research assistant in the Hyperbaric Physiology Laboratory, of which he was the director. In a typical mentoring relationship, the mentor usually sets the tone for the experience. However, this was not the case with Dr. Fife and me. He created an office for me that adjoined his. He did not schedule specific times to meet with me for progress updates, nor did he have a specific agenda; he left it up to me to consult with him when I needed to. This is probably a result of his observing me to be independent, assertive, and, to a certain degree, self-reliant.

In all my classes for the master's degree program, I was the only black graduate student and, more often than not, the only black female. Since my disciplinary area was human physiology and since the Department of Biology did not have a formal program in that area, most of my classes were taken at the Texas A&M University College of Veterinary Medicine. I did not find this experience to be alien or uncomfortable. After much reflection, the only conclusion that I can come to is that, while the environment was indeed predominantly white, my cultural experiences as a product of the mainstream culture in the Caribbean made my academic and social experiences in and out of the classroom successful. As a matter of fact, I experienced much more culture shock moving from a melting-pot high school in Jamaica to a historically black university than in making the transition from a historically black university to a predominantly white university. My experiences in the latter setting were mostly positive ones.

In the spring of 1986 I was accepted into the college teaching doctoral program in the Department of Curriculum and Instruction. Before my acceptance in the program, I met Dr. Glenn Ross Johnson, chairperson of the College Teaching Program and director of the Texas A&M University Center for Teaching Excellence. After my first semester, he agreed to be the chairperson for my dissertation committee. My mentoring experiences in the Department of Curriculum and Instruction were somewhat different now from those I had had with Dr. Fife, and on a new level compared to those in the Department of Biology. My mentoring experiences with Dr. Johnson began during my internship with the Center for Teaching Excellence. Dr. Johnson had the idea of hiring graduate students who were nearing the completion of the College Teaching Program, and who were prepared in a discipline outside of education, to serve as instructional specialists at the center. It was through the College Teaching Program, my experience as a teaching assistant, and this internship that I was introduced to faculty development.

Dr. Johnson's role, in addition to guiding and advising, was one of counseling. He supported and encouraged me throughout all my endeavors and provided a lot of latitude from which to grow and develop my skills. It was during my Ph.D. degree program that I became actively involved in university-wide student organizations such as the Graduate Student Council, the Caribbean Students Association, and the International Students Association, where I held leadership positions as vice-president, president, and president, respectively. Because of my mentoring experiences, the avenues I had traveled, and my experience with these organizations, I also became a mentor for minority undergraduate and graduate students.

I found myself mentoring undergraduate students about graduate school in my office. For some of my Caribbean peers, my office at the Center for Teaching Excellence became a haven of sorts in which to relax or talk between classes. My active mentoring experiences ranged from active listening or tutoring, assisting with a paper or project, to simply pointing someone in the right direction. An experience that holds fond memories for me is when I was invited to give the welcome address at the Beta Beta Beta Biological Honor Society, Sigma Chi Chapter, induction banquet at Prairie View A&M University. I spoke to the undergraduates on the importance of extracurricular activities in helping to create a balance between academic and social growth.

Like Dr. Fife, Dr. Johnson at times demanded high levels of achievement from me and was always nurturing in our dialogues. Both individuals included me in informal activities such as lunch, discussion following meetings and lectures, social and departmental gatherings at their homes, and participation in academic conferences. They were very willing and sincere in providing support to people different from themselves. In my case, they were able to cross the boundaries of race, gender, and culture in working with me as a protégé. I recall a particular instance when, weeks after successfully defending my dissertation, I experienced "postdissertation syndrome." I was depressed and overly critical of myself, wondering if I would ever find a job. Dr. Johnson "cornered" me one morning in the hallway and said, "Let's go for a walk." Throughout our walk, which lasted for almost an hour, he counseled me to be patient, while recounting his own experiences as a graduate student. He assured me that things would improve and that it would only be a matter of time before I found the job I wanted. He was right. Two weeks later I began interviewing for faculty development positions and was appointed to the position I am currently holding at Ohio State University.

The relationships between myself and Dr. Fife, and myself and Dr. Johnson, are special ones. Having more than one mentor helped me to expand a variety of social and professional networks and also to create allies and alliances. They are largely responsible for having molded me into the professional that I am today. Since Dr. Fife also served as the outside faculty representative on my dissertation committee, the mentoring relationship between us continued throughout both graduate degree programs. Since both my mentors were white males, one might ask if the situation would have been different, or more desirable, if I had had female and/or black mentors. I honestly do not know; however, I suspect that there are gender-related differences in mentoring relationships.

With Dr. Fife and Dr. Johnson, I never felt the need to have a female or minority mentor, or even wondered what the racial or gender difference would have been like if I had such an individual to turn to. For me, those factors were irrelevant. I did establish a mentoring relationship with Dr. Julia Clark, a black female professor in the Department of Curriculum and Instruction, toward the end of my doctoral degree program. She served on my dissertation committee and assisted me in navigating through the nuances of departmental politics. The mentoring relationship here, however, was different from the encounters with Drs. Fife and Johnson.

There is no doubt that the mentoring experience is complex. It involves a myriad of factors and the relationship between mentor and protégé varies from one encounter to the next. For some students, and for me in particular, the various levels involved in the experience contribute greatly to professional, intellectual, and social development. Having a strong support system, such as a mentor or mentors, the department, the college, and the university, is very important in finding a secure medium that will encourage one to grow, develop, and learn in a diverse university community.

*CHRISTINE A. STANLEY is instructional development specialist in the Office of Faculty and TA Development at the Center for Instructional Resources, The Ohio State University, Columbus.*

# A Checklist for Developing, Implementing, and Assessing Mentoring Programs

Mentoring works. Participants and institutions benefit. Mentoring will continue to enrich, enliven, and affect student and faculty development now and in the future. Some chapter authors of this volume discussed their attempts to conceptualize, define, develop, implement, and assess mentoring programs in their institutions. Others provided insights into the human side of the mentoring process. While all mentoring programs have a common core of values and a commitment to help people develop their full potential and advance in educational and professional paths, *we know that there is no one way to accomplish these goals.* However, we do have sufficient evidence from the literature, research, and model programs to understand that certain basic elements must be present to make mentoring programs effective. In addition to being based on solid planning and provided with sufficient resources, mentoring programs must fit into the institutional culture, meet the needs of participants and sponsors, become integrated into the support services network, and validate and highlight their achievements.

As institutions change, as student and faculty demographics shift, as barriers to equitable advancement are broken, mentoring will evolve new goals and structures. Rather than being a definitive summary of what mentoring is or should be, the following checklist is designed to serve as a guide for those who wish to consider structured mentoring programs as an answer to the development of human resources in any institution. The checklist is not intended to be definitive or proscriptive, but instead to serve as a stimulus to asking the kind of institution-based questions necessary to launch and implement a comprehensive mentoring program.

## Assessing Individual and Institutional Needs for Mentoring

Why do we want a mentoring program?
What specific needs will it address?
How were these needs determined (for example, by a special study, administrative mandate, identification of a problem, requests from potential users)?

Is mentoring an appropriate activity to meet these needs?
Does the institutional mission support this kind of activity?
Does the institutional development plan articulate these goals?
Do the campus climate and culture value this activity?
Are there existing programs that are potential collaborators or competitors?
Is this the right time to begin a formal program?
Are there any barriers to establishing a mentoring program?

## Defining Goals and Outcomes for Mentoring

How is mentoring to be defined for your program?
Who will determine the program goals (for example, the administration, an advisory group, or the participants)?
Are these short- or long-term goals?
What are the measurable outcomes for participants?
Are there stated outcomes for the institution?
Who will determine when goals are met?

## Positioning the Program in the Organization

Who will act as sponsors, patrons, or advocates of the program?
Which position/office will be responsible for the program?
Does this unit have sufficient power, influence, and resources to support the program?
Is mentoring to be considered an academic or a service program?
What are the implications of this decision?
Do you need an advisory committee?
What will be its role: planning, publicity, advocacy?
Will it be a campuswide program? A departmental program? A program for a target group (for example, minority students, women faculty, nontraditional students, new faculty, women in science, minority students in engineering, and so on)?
Will the mentoring program be part of other initiatives (for example, student counseling, faculty development, or minority programs)?
How will the program be announced and publicized?

## Determining and Obtaining Program Resources

What resources are needed to accomplish program goals in terms of staff, time, space, and materials?
Who is responsible for obtaining resources? By what process?
Will resources be temporary or permanent?
Will funds come from internal or external sources?
Will there be supplemental funds from grants?

Is the program expected to generate funds?

Will an operating budget be designated for the program?

Who determines the amount of the budget and the allowable expenditures?

What staff is needed and how will it be acquired: by hire, by loan, through volunteering, or through release time?

How much and what kind of space is required for mentoring activities?

How central and accessible is the program office for users?

## Developing and Coordinating the Program

How much planning time is required before the program begins for needs assessment, hiring staff, preparing materials, publicity?

Will the program follow the calendar or the academic year?

At what point will activities begin?

What activities will constitute a mentoring program: pairing mentors/mentees, mentoring groups, orientations, training sessions for participants, counseling, social activities, tutoring?

How will the program activities be organized and scheduled?

How much structure or flexibility do you need to meet goals?

Who will be responsible for coordinating the program?

What qualifications will the coordinator need?

How much time will the coordinator give to the program?

Where will the program and coordinator be physically located?

## Selecting and Monitoring Participants

How will participants be identified?

How will mentors be selected: volunteers, solicited, referred?

How will mentors be screened: for age, ethnicity, skills, attitudes, values, gender, or what feature(s)?

What expectations will be set for participation in terms of time commitment, meetings, reports, and so on?

How will they be trained to be effective?

Will mentors be compensated or rewarded for participation?

How will mentees be selected? Will they be volunteers, will they be referred, or will they be part of special programs?

What expectations will be set for mentees?

How will mentors and mentees be matched: by age, ethnicity, gender, academic discipline, or what other criteria?

Have you assessed the advantages and disadvantages of different kinds of matches: cross-gender, same discipline, same gender, and so on?

Who will do the matching?

Will individuals have a choice in pairing?

Will individuals have options if the match is not compatible?

Have you considered the potential problem areas in matching (for example, sexual harassment)?

How will the coordinator interact with the pairs?

Will the pairs interact with other pairs?

What will be the duration of the match?

When does the formal mentoring conclude?


## Assessing the Program

Why do you need to evaluate the program?

Is evaluation required for administrative support, to validate success, to obtain program data, to get feedback from participants?

When you determine the purpose for assessment, how will you choose the types of evaluation to be used?

Can you use standard methodology, or will you want to develop special forms and methods?

Do you need immediate, short-term feedback from participants?

Will this be used for program development or changes?

Do you need long-term assessment of program impact?

Do you have a plan to acquire data as the program proceeds?

Do you have the expertise to evaluate the program?

Will assessment data be available for research on the program?

Who has access to program data and for what activities?

Will you publish an annual report on the program?


What other questions and issues are crucial to your particular institution?

# INDEX

Adams, M., 74
African-Americans, 101, 102
Aisenberg, N., 53
Alleman, E., 30
Armstrong-West, S., 36
Ash, R. A., 19
Assessment, 32, 33
Astin, A., 4
Atwater, C., 12, 33, 53, 54, 57
Austin, A. E., 66, 67

Bahniuk, M. H., 94
Baldwin, R. G., 65
Bardwick, J., 92
*Barriers to Retention and Tenure: The Experiences of Faculty Cohorts,* 54
Berquist, W. H., 4, 11
Biocultural, 118–119
Blackburn, R. T., 12
Blackwell, J., 102
Boice, R., 12, 30, 32, 33, 55, 65, 73, 81, 83, 85, 95
Bolton, B., 28
Bourguignon, E., 53
Brewton-Parker College. *See* Freshman Mentoring Program (Brewton-Parker College)
Brown, R. D., 28, 37
Bryant, G., 16
Burke, R. J., 16
Byer, K. D., 94

Cameron, S., 12
Career stages, mentoring relationship and: beginning career, 19–20; midcareer, 20–21
Carmin, C. N., 2, 32, 33
Carroll, J., 93
Centra, J. A., 79
Chao, G. T., 36
Chapman, D., 12
Cheerleader, mentor as, 28
Clark, J. C., 125
Coach and confidant relationship, 28
Cochran, J., 30
Collins, N. W., 18

Color, graduate students of, 101–103; personal narratives of peer mentoring, 103–110; reflections on advantages of peer mentoring approach, 110–111
Colorado State University, 86
Compensation, for mentors, 31
Cotton, J. L., 18
Counselor, mentor as, 28
Creswell, J. W., 93, 94
Cullen, D. L., 85
Cultivation phase, mentoring relationship, 22
Cultural mentoring, 115–118

Daloz, L. A., 79, 94
Darrow, C. M., 1, 12, 15, 17, 19, 20, 28, 91
Davies, A., 102
DeCoster, D. A., 28
DeFour, D. C., 29, 30
de la Teja, M. H., 36
Departmental faculty mentoring, 81–82; aspects of, 82–84; "do-nothing" approach, 89; institutionally mandated approach, 88–89; principles of, 84–85; "soft-sell" approach, 86–88
Diehl, P. F., 68
Dingerson, M., 53
Discrimination, 17
Dobos, J., 94
Douthitt, R. A., 53
Doverspike, J., 30
Dreher, G. F., 19
Duane, J., 76, 95
Duggar, M., 28

East Carolina University, 88
Edgerton, Russell, 79
Egly, N. M., 94
Elman, N. S., 36
Endo, J. J., 36
Erickson, B. L., 76
Erickson, G. R., 76
Evaluation, of mentoring outcomes, 32–33
Eveslage, S. A., 53
Exum, W. H., 53

Shulman, C. H., 73
Shuster, J. H., 12, 93, 97
Simpson, R. D., 68
Sleeter, C. E., 11
Sponsors, 28
Stage, F., 53
Steele, C., 102
Stone, T. E., 73
Stonewater, B., 53
Swoboda, M. J., 28

Teacher, mentor as, 28
Teaching, mentoring new faculty for, 65–66
Teaching Improvement Program (TIP): impact of the program, 70; program activities, 69–70; selecting mentors, 68–69
Terenzini, P. T., 12, 28, 36
Terrell, M. C., 2, 12, 28, 35
Texas A&M, 121–125
Thomas Rivera Center for Policy Studies on Latino Issues, 102
Tinto, V., 35
Titus, P., 28, 29, 30
Tompkins, J., 9, 10, 12
Turner, J. L., 83, 85

Undergraduate minority students program model, 35–37; marketing, 39–40; method, 37–38; program activities, 39; program goals, 38; program participants, 38–39; retention data, 40
Unilateral contracts, 92

University of Georgia (UGA), 66, 67
University of Hawaii, 54, 55, 56
University of Maryland University College (UMUC), 73; colleagues helping colleagues, 75–77; overview of peer mentoring at, 74–75; peer mentor process, 77–78; peer mentors, 78–79; setting of, 74
University of Nebraska, 96

Waite, B., 28
Walz, P. M., 36
Weimer, M. G., 75
Wheeler, D. W., 12, 93, 94, 96, 97
Wilson, J., 36
Wilson, R., 78
Women: importance of mentoring for, 17–18; minority, 58
Women junior faculty mentoring program, 53–54; activities of, 58–59; assessment, 59–60; beginnings of, 54–55; goals of, 55–56; institutional impact of, 60–61; pairings, 56–57; structure of, 55; training, 57
Wright, C. A., 17
Wright, D. J., 2, 12, 35
Wright, S. D., 17
Wrightsman, L. S., 32
Wunsch, M. A., 30, 33, 59

Yoder, J. D., 53

Zey, M. G., 28

# ORDERING INFORMATION

NEW DIRECTIONS FOR TEACHING AND LEARNING is a series of paperback books that presents ideas and techniques for improving college teaching, based both on the practical expertise of seasoned instructors and on the latest research findings of educational and psychological researchers. Books in the series are published quarterly in spring, summer, fall, and winter and are available for purchase by subscription as well as by single copy.

SUBSCRIPTIONS for 1994 cost $47.00 for individuals (a savings of 25 percent over single-copy prices) and $62.00 for institutions, agencies, and libraries. Please do not send institutional checks for personal subscriptions. Standing orders are accepted.

SINGLE COPIES cost $15.95 when payment accompanies order. (California, New Jersey, New York, and Washington, D.C., residents please include appropriate sales tax.) Billed orders will be charged postage and handling.

DISCOUNTS FOR QUANTITY ORDERS are available. Please write to the address below for information.

ALL ORDERS must include either the name of an individual or an official purchase order number. Please submit your order as follows:
*Subscriptions:* specify series and year subscription is to begin
*Single copies:* include individual title code (such as TL54)

MAIL ALL ORDERS TO:
Jossey-Bass Publishers
350 Sansome Street
San Francisco, CA 94104-1342

FOR SINGLE-COPY SALES OUTSIDE OF THE UNITED STATES, CONTACT:
Maxwell Macmillan International Publishing Group
866 Third Avenue
New York, NY 10022-6221

FOR SUBSCRIPTION SALES OUTSIDE OF THE UNITED STATES, CONTACT:
any international subscription agency or Jossey-Bass directly.

OTHER TITLES AVAILABLE IN THE
NEW DIRECTIONS FOR TEACHING AND LEARNING SERIES
*Robert J. Menges*, Editor-in-Chief
*Marilla D. Svinicki*, Associate Editor